Program Guide

Getting Along with Others

Teaching Social Effectiveness to Children

Nancy F. Jackson

Donald A. Jackson

Cathy Monroe

Research Press / 2612 North Mattis Avenue / Champaign Illinois 61821

15 14 13 12 11 10 9 8   94 95 96 97

Research and program development efforts leading to the creation of these materials were supported, in part,
by Grant No. G007804996 from the Office of Special Education, U.S. Department of Education,
through Children's Behavioral Services in Reno, Nevada.
However, these materials do not necessarily represent the policy of the Federal Government,
and no endorsement by it should be assumed.

Copies of this book may be ordered from the publisher at the address given on the title page.

ISBN 0-87822-269-3
ISBN 0-87822-270-7 (2-volume set)

Library of Congress Catalog Card Number 82-62611

Contents

List of Activities

Preface

SOCIAL SKILLS TRAINING programs are needed because many children do not acquire critically important social abilities without them. Depending upon how the problem is defined, deficit social skills may be causally related to poor school performance, juvenile delinquency, adult psychopathology, etc. Social skills-building is based on the assumption that problems of adjustment are related to a lack of certain social abilities and that a correction or a learning of these skills will reduce the occurrence of more serious problems (see review of the literature under "Importance of Social Skills Instruction" in Chapter 1).

Interest in social behavior *per se* is certainly not new. Current work in this area is building upon decades of previous research. What is new is the attention to systematic training approaches that provide for the introduction and mastery of individual skills in a supportive environment and generalization of skills to critical settings. This approach takes the position that the most straightforward treatment is to simply *tell* the person what to do in situations identified as problematic; to *show* the person how to do it; and to have the person *practice* the new skill before having to use it in real life. Teachers and others working with children can then take advantage of every opportunity to teach or strengthen skills.

Getting Along With Others: Teaching Social Effectiveness to Children is a program that combines the wisdom of the direct intervention approach with systematic instructional techniques. The result is a package that (1) creates a setting for introducing and practicing new skills systematically and (2) provides the tools for maximizing the potential for learning social skills during spontaneous interactions. Teachers and others who facilitate children's acquisition of social skills will find here a technology that is simple to learn and yet extremely effective, a technology that simultaneously teaches social skills and provides for behavior management in group settings. Anyone who is faced with the task of managing the behavior of groups of children so they may benefit from academic, recreational, or social events should find this technology useful in creating a more effective and positive environment.

Throughout this Program Guide an assumption is made that the user is working with elementary-aged children. This emphasis reflects the interests and original experiences of the developers. However, it needs to be made clear that, with appropriate modifications, the program has been used successfully with a variety of populations. Specifically, the incidental teaching strategies have been applied in preschool settings; this and other program components have been used by teachers, psychologists, counselors, and others working with youngsters from first grade through high school age; and the entire program has been implemented in a variety of settings with elementary and middle school children with serious social adjustment and special education needs, and with mildly retarded people between the ages of 18 and 35. Of course, if you intend to use the lessons and other activities with someone other than elementary children, you will need to make changes to ensure relevancy of role plays and examples.

The program techniques might be summed up in three main categories: (1) a method for determining personal expectations of social behavior and for breaking behaviors into learnable components; (2) a method for delivering instruction of new skills; and (3) methods for managing children's social behavior and for taking advantage of the social learning potential in ongoing interactions with children.

There are two main parts to this package to train and assist you in the implementation of the program. The first is the *Program Guide*. This will take you through a step-by-step process of learning about the program and how to use its various components. The second part is *Skill Lessons and Activities*, which provides lessons for the 17 core social skills taught in the demonstration groups, as well as other materials that were used in the demonstration groups, including relaxation scripts, group activities for strengthening each new social skill, and Homework and Home Notes for each skill.

For further assistance in learning the program, color videotapes are available from the authors, prepared specifically for training new program users. This series of five tapes, called *Social Effectiveness Training: Positive Interactions for Success with Children*,* provides models of each teaching skill and of the program's small-group social skills training format. Although these tapes are optional, they provide an extremely useful addition to the written materials.

These training materials represent the contributions and conscientious work of many people, in particular some who lived the program and found ways to make it better or to effectively teach it to others. Lisa Stone, Barbara Jensen, and Candy Wilkins nurtured the program from its inception through its maturation and saw it through many growing pains. Many other talented people made important contributions to the refinement of the program. A very special thanks goes to Donna Aukai, Joyce Meyer, Cheryl Purvis, Allan Reinap, and Marty Waltz. Their creativity, patience, and good humor are gratefully acknowledged.

*Jackson, N.F., Monroe, C., and Jackson, D.A. (Producers). *Social effectiveness training: Positive interactions for success with children.* Available from the authors, Social Effectiveness Training, P.O. Box 6664, Reno, Nev. 89513.

We cannot resist a final note here, since a more appropriate opportunity may never occur. The years spent with the program have been unique among our professional and personal experiences. We succeeded at pulling together a powerful group of people, each with his or her own unique talents and contributions. Living with and amongst these professionals has been an extremely rewarding experience, and our individual growing and changing could not help but have an impact on the program. But that's another story. You will undoubtedly find, however, that these materials reflect our desire to discover what we need in order to make our lives positive and rewarding, and then to do what is necessary to make them that way.

NANCY F. JACKSON
DONALD A. JACKSON, PH.D.
CATHY MONROE
JANUARY, 1983

Chapter 1

Previewing the Program

Before you invest your time and energy in this program, you should know what you are getting into. What is reasonable to expect of these materials? What is expected of you as a learner?

This Program Guide provides the information and training activities you need to learn to implement an effective program of instruction in social skills. You will learn to use two types of procedures: techniques for interacting with children that can make each social encounter an episode for teaching social skills and tightly organized skill introduction sequences. Each of these instructional modes is important, and together they form a powerful intervention strategy for introducing skills and ensuring their general use. Many users of the program have described how effective it has been for them. We are confident that you, too, will find these techniques useful.

In the next few pages you will read background information on the program. The purpose of this chapter is to describe the underlying assumptions of the program, the problems motivating the development of systematic social skills instruction, the program in overview, its results, and the objectives of this Program Guide. Chapter 2 provides an overview of the type and length of each training activity you will complete in learning to use the materials. We suggest that you review these sections so that you can make a well-informed decision to spend your time and energy on this training.

If you study the Program Guide and complete all the suggested tasks, you should be well on your way to implementing the program. Yet the materials *per se* lack the element most important to the success of the program: your commitment of the time and energy necessary to learn it. That part is up to you.

Underlying Assumptions

Underlying most innovative approaches is a philosophy, a theoretical or methodological base for the original hypothesis that the approach will work. It is important that such assumptions be explicit. This is especially true when the approach is meant for adoption by people from various backgrounds and when the success of adoptions is likely to be correlated with the extent to which adopters embrace and commit themselves to the approach. Therefore,

a prerequisite to your further pursuit of the training is exposure to the basic philosophy of the program.

The first major premise of the program is that the style with which the instructor interacts with the children has a dramatic impact on their acquisition of new skills. What is the style of the program? It's probably best described as extremely positive, with the focus on specific characteristics of interactional responses. **The primary philosophy is that all interactions are opportunities for children to improve their social behavior and to receive support and positive consequences for doing so.**

Another important assumption is that many children have not learned vital skills for success in social interactions – their difficulties are based in a skill deficit which exists independently from or along with other emotional or cognitive problems. Skill in one's social environments under normal conditions is a product of learning through antecedent and consequent stimuli that, through their informational and motivational qualities, steer one toward certain response sets and away from others. For example, one imitates models of effective social behavior and repeats responses that produce the acknowledgment and encouragement of others. When these natural events do not work to teach social skills due to poor models, lack of reinforcement, or the inability of the learner, an explicit social skills training technology becomes relevant. Then, the usual hidden social skills curriculum is inadequate; we must program learning at the learner's level. Thus, the mode of treatment offered by this program is *instructional*, a model for *teaching* new skills.

Another important assumption underlying this program's approach is that its scope is necessarily limited. That is, the instructional strategies used here are based on a skill deficit model; other possible treatment modes are not used. Social behavioral problems are usually addressed by practitioners with training in psychology; to many, this implies a counseling model. This program should be seen as distinct and separate from (though not incompatible with) counseling. The user of this program becomes instructor, not counselor, with the primary goal of teaching new behaviors. This does not mean that the same user cannot, at another time, take on the role of counselor and address a separate set of goals. It does mean that it is important not to mix these roles during the use of the program; responding to more than one set of priorities can cause the instructor to seem inconsistent and confuse the children.

Educational technology provides useful strategies for efficiently and effectively teaching new skills. These strategies are used here to teach the components of new social skills in a nonthreatening situation before they are attempted under stress. Yet social environments will have a much greater impact than any contrived training experience, and research clearly shows that behavior is situation specific and often quite resistant to generalizing. Thus, this program emphasizes the incidental teaching of social skills within natural environments or in social situations created specifically for conducting incidental teaching. The assumption is that a pragmatic approach is best; being flexible enough to learn and refine your approach based on what you observe is essential.

Importance of Social Skills Instruction

Social skills development under normal conditions is a product of various factors that occur unpredictably in a child's life. As with any complex skill developed without the benefit of systematic instruction, problems often arise. Children who are deprived of opportunities to learn may be left with skill deficits.

Social skills deficiencies become especially problematic when a child begins attending school. Teachers face the reality that in addition to academics, social skills must be taught, since instruction is impossible without them. Social skills training is the hidden curriculum in the classroom, and there is an urgent need to make it explicit.

Skills Deficits

Although the connection between social skills deficits and more severe psychopathology has long been established (e.g., Zigler & Phillips, 1961), the development of systematic social skills training programs has occurred only recently. Fortunately, research and demonstration programs are showing that it is possible to create an explicit social skills training technology for educators and other professionals concerned with providing instruction and treatment for children.

The need for social skills training for children is supported through investigations showing that interaction skills deficits can be related to a wide array of presenting problems (Gambrill, 1977). For example, social isolation in children has been associated with high rates of juvenile delinquency (Roff, Sells, & Golden, 1972), bad conduct military discharges (Ross, 1976), dropping out of school (Ullmann, 1957), and mental health problems (Cowen, Pederson, Babigian, Izzo, & Trost, 1973; Zigler & Phillips, 1961). Early aggression has been related to academic failure (Kornrich, 1965), alcoholism (Schilder, 1941), and antisocial behavior (Morris, 1956). On the other hand, researchers have related high social status in childhood to academic achievement (Laughlin, 1954; Porterfield & Schlichting, 1961) and good adjustment in adulthood (Barclay, 1966; Guinouard & Rychlak, 1962).

The development of social abilities in children and adolescents has been studied by many researchers. Deficits in social skills have largely been attributed to deficient learning histories, anxiety, or lack of opportunity to use and practice social responses. Social skills training, then, involves the teaching of responses that can help to improve one's ability in interpersonal situations (Hersen & Bellack, 1977).

Interventions

The research literature, especially during the last 15 years, has reported on a variety of interventions to change social behavior in children. Generally, these studies agree that (a) the arrangement of antecedent and contingent events in the child's environment can produce important changes in identified social behaviors and that (b) training in specific social skills can be accomplished by means of such procedures as modeling, behavioral rehearsal, feedback, and practice. Various reviews of the relevant literature support these conclusions (Cartledge & Milburn, 1980; Hops & Greenwood, 1981; Van Hasselt, Hersen, Whitehill, & Bellack, 1979). In particular, Van Hasselt et al. (1979) made the point that when a child lacks specific social skills that are needed to be effective in social situations, it is not appropriate to simply apply reinforcing contingencies. Rather, a combination of instruction in the missing skills with such contingencies is needed. A problem frequently noted is the generalization of newly trained skills to significant environments (Berler, Gross, & Drabman, 1982; Cooke & Apolloni, 1976; LaGreca & Santogrossi, 1980). Especially since training is often conducted away from a child's natural environment, ways to enhance generalization should be carefully incorporated into an intervention plan.

Thus, there is considerable evidence on the kinds of procedures that will produce change in social behavior, and on areas of concern that training programs must address. This program incorporates the lessons of research in the topic area to create a social skills training package adaptable to a variety of training settings with children.

The Demonstration Project: Social Effectiveness Training

In 1976 work was begun on social effectiveness training for elementary-aged children. Based on initial efforts made with the assistance of a small grant from the Nevada Department of Education, a "Handicapped Children's Model Program" proposal was submitted in 1978 and funded by the U.S. Department of Education. The program was initially developed at a community mental health center; thus, some of the parameters of the demonstration model were created especially for this setting. In this context children met in groups of six to eight, with two instructors. Each biweekly session lasted for 2 hours and focused on one or two specific skills. The daily schedule consisted of the following:

15 minutes: **Free Play**. Period of free play for those who brought Homework completed satisfactorily; time to practice and do Homework on the last skill taught for those who did not bring Homework

10 minutes: **Review of Homework**. Public acknowledgment (in the group) for those who had done the Homework

10 minutes: **Relaxation Training**. A series of relaxation exercises designed to gradually teach children to relax in progressively more real and stressful situations

30 minutes: **Lesson**. Introduction of the new skill using the structured Skill Lesson Format, including demonstration by teachers and ample role play opportunities for children

20 minutes: **Snack Time**. Refreshments (contingent on demonstrating competence in new skills and rule following), providing opportunities for social interaction and use of conversation skills

20 minutes: **Activity**. Games, art projects, and other activities to provide high-risk settings in which skills such as compromising, sharing, and problem solving may be practiced

15 minutes: **Home Notes**. Time for filling out Home Notes together to review the day's objectives and each child's target behaviors and make opportunities for approval and Positive Feedback from peers

This format blended highly structured and less structured activities so that training could occur on two important levels: children were introduced to new skills in a systematic manner and then given ample opportunities to behave spontaneously, using new skills with guidance and support from the teachers. The less structured activities also made it more likely that referral problems and target behaviors would occur so that they could be treated.

During the structured lesson time children were guided through practice trials with the new skill until they were completely successful. This guaranteed that each child *could* use the skill; the trick was to ensure that the child *would* use it in routine interactions with

people. To promote this generalization, we coupled direct instruction with incidental teaching. That is, all of the child's spontaneous behavior was used as instructional material; ongoing interactions resulted either in support from the teacher or guidance via corrective feedback, practice, and support. Activities such as snack, free play, games, and art projects allowed the child to behave as much as possible like she would in school, home, or neighborhood settings. If the program were conducted within the setting where the problems occur (where there are ample opportunities for incidental teaching), there would be little or no need to have support activities (e.g., snack time) scheduled especially for social skills training. If the program were taught in the classroom, for example, normally occurring events would provide perfect social skills training situations, so such activities as snack time might not be necessary.

By the end of 1981 the program had been introduced into a variety of new settings by various professionals trained to use it. These program adopters were able to replicate both the form and the results of the original program. Uses ranged from a number of careful replications of the small-group model (children were released from their regular classroom to attend a 2-hour group with two counselors and/or teachers acting as program instructors) to the use of the program's techniques and formats in regular elementary classrooms (a teacher and 30 children in a self-contained classroom). Training in the program had been requested and provided to a variety of professionals in school, mental health, mental retardation, day care, university, and community college settings. Adaptations had been carried into special and regular classrooms (kindergarten through high school), rural and urban mental health centers, counseling sessions by school counselors and psychologists, social skills training groups offered privately, day care centers, group homes for retarded individuals, and parent-child or sibling interactions in family settings. These experiences confirmed that the program was acceptable and useful to adopters in various settings (see Jackson, Jackson, & Monroe, 1981).

Essence of the Program

The program package provides the practitioner with a complete technology for efficiently adding social skills training to the existing classroom curriculum or clinical program with minimal disruption to the setting. Factors which make this package particularly effective and efficient include the skill breakdowns, the instructional format for introducing new skills, and the carefully analyzed Teaching Strategies. Each of the 17 socially validated skills is defined in terms of its specific behavioral components. Thus, presentation and demonstration of the skill may be accomplished without ambiguity, and follow-up support for and refinement of the skill may be consistent. Presentation of the various skills is organized such that one skill builds upon another. Basic classroom survival skills are introduced first to pave the way and help the children develop the necessary behaviors to facilitate learning more sophisticated interactional skills.

According to feedback from those trained in the use of the package, by far one of the most valuable aspects is learning the five Teaching Strategies, which are based on the analysis and refinement of exemplary teaching as well as findings of current research in psychology and education. These teaching techniques are categorized and broken into components for easy learning.

This systematic social skills curriculum includes a built-in behavior management system and provides a way of delivering ongoing social skills instruction while reducing or eliminating problem social behaviors. The Teaching Strategies provide the opportunity to turn power struggles with children into positive outcomes. These core Teaching Strategies become a behavioral repertoire from which an instructor can choose an option that will fit most any learning situation. In fact, the five core Teaching Strategies and the lesson plan content define 75% of the interactions between children and their instructors who have been trained in this program. This statistic is based on observational data taken during instruction. A few other useful teaching skills define virtually the rest of the interactions. Thus, the options in any given interactional situation are clear. The program provides you with training in using each of the Teaching Strategies, including scripts for typical interactional vignettes. In any setting the Teaching Strategies provide a continuum of options, ranging from interactions which rely on the child to take major responsibility for behaving on his own to more teacher-directed interactions. After training, you will be able to assess the actual situations which arise, determine the priorities for the child, and choose the most effective approach.

Effectiveness of the Program

Repeated uses of the program have demonstrated its effectiveness with most children receiving the training. As of this writing, the program developers have conducted nearly 40 training groups. In addition, instructors trained by the program developers have conducted approximately 10 groups, and numerous teachers have learned the basic program and adapted parts of it to their special education or regular classrooms.

As expected, greater success has resulted with chil-

dren determined *a priori* to be appropriate for social skills training. In general, children with very minor or very severe problems and children primarily exhibiting motivational problems were not as successful in the program as were children who clearly had skill deficits in the areas targeted. (Also see discussion on screening children in Chapter 7.)

Reviewing Evaluations of the Demonstration Groups

The training sessions required that the children demonstrate their ability to use the skill being trained before being dismissed to reinforcing activities. Thus, all children met their individualized criteria for each skill trained within the sessions. Of greater interest and importance were indicators showing that following training, children spontaneously used the skills under natural conditions. For this reason, program evaluations stressed the social validation of training results.

Several reports of the program's outcomes have been made. Evaluations included telephone interviewing before, during, and after training (Jackson, 1982), taped naturalistic observations before and after training (Jackson, Jackson, Monroe, & Wilkins, 1979), and several types of behavior ratings (Jackson, Jackson, Monroe, & Wilkins, 1980). For example, a standardized parent rating scale called the Louisville Behavior Checklist or LBC (Miller, 1977) was repeatedly used before and again after training. Nineteen scales provided measures of social and emotional adjustment in children ages 4 to 13. Among the 10 scales relevant to the program are AG-Aggression (a composite scale including items describing demanding, belligerent, impulsive, or destructive behaviors) and IN-Inhibition (a composite scale including items describing social isolation, "unlikeableness," and fear). Improvements have been consistently obtained on the LBC for children trained with the program. Before training, the scores on targeted scales usually fell in the significant problem range (greater than 1 standard deviation from the community average); scores following training fell well within the normal range. This difference was found consistently for almost all children trained in the program groups. When several children waiting to enter the program were scored on the LBC at 90-day intervals without training, this improvement was not noted.

The extent to which others perceived a change in children's social skills following training was also checked using the program's 25-item Consumer Satisfaction Scale (Appendix A) that allowed teachers and parents to rate their satisfaction with the child's social abilities on a Likert scale from 1 (completely dissatisfied) to 7 (completely satisfied). Parents' satisfaction ratings before training averaged "slightly dissatisfied," while after training they were in the satisfied range. Teachers on the average tended to be more neutral before training but also reported improvements after training.

Reviewing Data from Replication Groups

The effectiveness of the model has also been indicated by evaluations of children in replication groups run by practitioners adopting the program. Results were obtained for 41 children trained in replication groups (four groups at a mental health center and two groups taught in elementary schools). Scores from the Louisville Behavior Checklist were similar to the results obtained in the demonstration groups (Jackson, 1982).

The usefulness and effectiveness of training professionals to use the program was also evaluated by checking participants' satisfaction with the quality of the training they received and the impact it had on their teaching methods and on children's social skills. Using a 7-point Likert scale, participants in instructor training expressed a high degree of satisfaction with the quality of the training they received. In addition, 25 of the 30 respondents (83%) indicated they were using the program procedures in work or home settings. The average ratings of the usefulness of the critical aspects of the program were all well within the "satisfied" range. A more complete description of procedures and effectiveness of training other professionals is reported elsewhere (Jackson, Jackson, & Monroe, 1981).

To directly assess the impact of the program on the teaching styles of trainees, eight participants were observed following training as they taught social skills with the program format. Teaching in pairs, the trainees taught four small groups of children in special education classrooms and school counseling settings. Three of the four pairs were found to be using the program's strategies in the same proportion as those prescribed and used by the program developers. That is, the core Teaching Strategies were used in about 75% of the interactions; other appropriate supplemental skills such as general praise were used in about 24% of the interactions; and only about 1% of the interactions included procedures not prescribed by the program (e.g., nagging, reminding, not praising appropriate behavior, arguing with a student, or giving answers without helping the student to figure it out himself). Although the fourth teaching pair completed the training, they did not consistently use the skills, and observations confirmed the program was not as well implemented. The proportions were: core skills, 50%; supplemental skills, 20%; nonprogram skills, 30%.

Use of the program's procedures appeared to directly relate to changes in students' behavior as well. The three pairs of training recipients who were found to be using the program's procedures correctly obtained improvements very similar to those obtained by the program's staff. For example, on the Louisville Behavior Checklist completed by parents, 10 scales measure behaviors relevant to our training. Of those scales with average scores within the "significant problem range" prior to our program's instruction, all but one moved into the "zone of desired outcomes" (within 1 standard deviation of the community mean) following instruction. For the students taught by the pair who did not consistently use the program's procedures, only one out of seven scales in the problem range moved into the desired outcome range (Jackson, Jackson, & Monroe, 1981).

Objectives

An important objective is providing flexibility for the user. It has been and will be repeatedly suggested that the program can mean a variety of things, depending upon the type of adoption or adaptation that fits the needs of your setting. If you are a regular elementary school teacher with a class of about 30 children, your use will undoubtedly differ from that of a psychologist in a local mental health center or even a counselor or special education teacher within your own school. This Program Guide attempts to address your differing training needs throughout, pointing out how various adaptations are possible.

The most important overall objective is to provide you with the skills and familiarity needed so that you can design and implement the best possible adapatation for your unique setting. Use of some program components is a must; some components are somewhat more flexible. Once you are familiar with *all* the components, you can design a plan for program use that includes the basics and whatever other elements you think will be practical and beneficial to you.

Completing the activities described in Chapter 2 should help you achieve the following *basic* goals for becoming competent in implementing this social effectiveness training program. Upon completing the tasks outlined, you will:

— Be well informed about the program—its philosophy, format, and effects.

— Demonstrate the ability to pinpoint incorrect social behavior and name the components of a positive alternative.

— Demonstrate the ability to use each of the five Teaching Strategies.

— Use the Skill Lesson Format to introduce new skills.

— Be familiar with necessary preparations to teach social skills in your setting.

Chapter 2

Using the Program Guide

Structure for Training

This Program Guide is structured for easy learning. You can enhance your study by using the videotape series, *Social Effectiveness Training: Positive Interactions for Success With Children* (see Preface for note about the videotape series). These materials provide what you will need to (1) become aware of concepts and strategies for teaching social skills, (2) engage in a step-by-step process that will result in mastery of the skills and procedures involved, and (3) obtain practice, evaluation, and feedback.

This Program Guide is intended to be the closest possible on-paper approximation to *in vivo* training. The videotapes help make the approximation a closer one, by modeling the use of the program. However, both inherently lack the elements which differentiate "book learning" from *in vivo* training. For example, our program workshops and courses have the advantage of offering peer pressure and support, lots of feedback, and even occasional snacks; it is relatively easy to ensure everyone's happiness, success, and motivation under these conditions. In using these materials without the assistance of an experienced program instructor, you will have to take responsibility for adding the elements that keep training fun and interesting. Be creative and good to yourself; schedule your time carefully and go through the training with at least one partner. One of our major goals is to perpetuate the use of the program package. Ensuring that you have positive, successful, and relatively painless experiences with it will help achieve that goal.

Importance of Role Playing

The Program Guide provides a number of activities for your learning experience. One of the most important of these is role playing. Although you may at first feel hesitant about role playing, you can overcome any shyness about it with a little effort. Feedback from program users has indicated that role playing has been the most valuable component of the training. In developing the program, we learned that discussion approaches do an excellent job of teaching learners how to *talk* about social skills, but very little to help them *establish* new social behaviors. To learn new ways of behaving, the learners must behave. Thus, we recommend that you – the learner at this point – take advantage of the opportunities to practice through role playing. The sequences involved in your own training before you begin teaching a group should prepare you to help the children to learn through role playing.

To facilitate your own role playing skills and to both practice and receive feedback and support, you will **need a partner.** Find someone who is also interested in learning to use the program and work through the Program Guide with that person. Only if you approach your training with at least one partner will you have the opportunity for all important practice and feedback.

Schedule for Training

The Program Guide prescribes training in two ways. First, you will independently complete activities such as reading, memorizing formats, and writing exercises. Second, you will need to schedule seven "class" meetings with your partner for discussion and problem solving, role playing, and feedback. Meeting weekly seems to work well; material learned stays fresh in your mind, and you should have plenty of time to complete assignments between meetings.

The checksheet and meeting agendas on the following pages are designed to structure your program training experience. Use the checksheet to help you schedule and then monitor your progress through the Program Guide. The seven meetings (1 hour each) and the preparatory exercises are outlined so that you will have clear step-by-step instructions for your training.

Activity 1. Scheduling Program Training

The Training Checksheet that follows gives step-by-step instructions for working through the Program Guide. **The seven meetings with your partner should be scheduled in advance. Meet with or call your partner** to decide on specific dates and times for the meetings and enter the information in the column titled Scheduled. Then, if you find it helpful, schedule times to complete the other activities on your own.

Training Checksheet

Task	Approximate Time	Scheduled (Date & Time)	Completed (Date)	Comments
Read: Chapter 1.	½ hour			

Read: Chapter 2.
Do: Activity:
  1: Scheduling Program Training
    (may be done with your partner by phone).
	½ hour			

Read: Chapter 3.
Do: Activity:
  2: Choosing Target Behaviors.
  3: Defining Target Behaviors.
  4: Defining Behaviors and Establishing Standards.
  5: Analyzing Situations.
	1 hour			

Meet: With partner. Complete Agenda for Meeting 1.	1 hour			

Read: Chapter 4 through Ignore-Attend-Praise only.
Do: Activity:
  6: Memorizing the Components
    (Positive Feedback).
  7: Right-Way Vignette for Positive Feedback.
  8: Discrimination Training for Positive Feedback.
11: Memorizing the Components
    (Ignore-Attend-Praise).
12: Right-Way Vignette for Ignore-Attend-Praise.
13: Discrimination Training for
    Ignore-Attend-Praise.
	1 hour			

Meet: With partner. Complete Agenda for Meeting 2.	1 hour			
Do: Activity: 10: Homework for Positive Feedback. 15: Homework for Ignore-Attend-Praise.	½ hour (write-up only)			

Read: Chapter 4 through the Direct Prompt.
Do: Activity:
16: Memorizing the Components (Teaching
    Interaction).
17: Right-Way Vignette for the Teaching Interaction.
18: Discrimination Training for the
    Teaching Interaction.
21: Memorizing the Components (Direct Prompt).
22: Right-Way Vignette for the Direct Prompt.
23: Discrimination Training for the Direct Prompt.
	1 hour			

Meet: With partner. Complete Agenda for Meeting 3.	1 hour			
Do: Activity: 20: Homework for the Teaching Interaction. 25: Homework for the Direct Prompt.	½ hour (write-up only)			
Read: Chapter 4 through the end. Do: Activity: 26: Memorizing the Components (Sit and Watch). 27: Right-Way Vignette for Sit and Watch. 28: Discrimination Training for Sit and Watch.	1 hour			
Meet: With partner. Complete Agenda for Meeting 4.	1 hour			
Do: Activity: 30: Homework for Sit and Watch.	10 minutes			
Read: Chapters 5 and 6. Do: Activity: 31: Memorizing the Skill Lesson Format.	1 hour			
Meet: With partner. Complete Agenda for Meeting 5.	1 hour			
Meet: With partner and others for Dry-Run Role Play. Complete Agenda for Meeting 6.	1 hour			
Read: Chapter 7.	½ hour			
Meet: With partner. Complete Agenda for Meeting 7.	1 hour			

Agendas for Training Meetings

Agenda for Meeting 1 (1 hour)

☐ Discuss Chapters 1, 2, and 3.

☐ Go over Activities 2, 3, 4, and 5. Discuss your social behavior standards.

Agenda for Meeting 2 (1 hour)

☐ Go over Activities 7, 8, 12, and 13. Discuss as needed.

☐ Do Activities 9 and 14. Give your partner feedback, using Evaluation Checksheets as needed. Activity 14 will require a third person or an "imaginary child."

Agenda for Meeting 3 (1 hour)

☐ Discuss Homework (Activities 10 and 15). Problem solve any difficulties you had implementing the skills.

☐ Go over Activities 17, 18, 22, and 23. Discuss as needed.

☐ Do Activities 19 and 24. Give your partner feedback, using Evaluation Checksheets as needed.

Agenda for Meeting 4 (1 hour)

☐ Discuss Homework (Activities 20 and 25).

☐ Go over Activities 27 and 28. Discuss as needed.

☐ Do Activity 29. Give your partner feedback, using Evaluation Checksheets as needed.

☐ Review the Teaching Interaction, role playing as needed.

☐ Discuss Guidelines for Using the Teaching Strategies, Additional Teaching Techniques, and Program Guidelines: Rules We Live By, from Chapter 4.

Agenda for Meeting 5 (1 hour)

☐ Discuss Homework (Activity 30).

☐ Do Activity 32.

☐ Discuss Chapter 5 if desired.

☐ Discuss Chapter 6. Decide if you want to try doing a "dry-run." If so, complete Activity 33.

Agenda for Meeting 6 (1 hour)

☐ Read instructions for Dry-Run Role Play and share with the volunteers, either verbatim or paraphrased.

☐ Discuss Behavior-Type Descriptions briefly.

☐ Pass out badges and Individual Instruction Sheets.

☐ Role play. Teach Following Directions, using the skill lesson from *Skill Lessons and Activities*.

☐ Discuss the role play.

Agenda for Meeting 7 (1 hour)

☐ Discuss Dry-Run Role Play experience. Provide your partner with feedback.

☐ Discuss issues raised by Chapter 7. Describe the logistics of using the program in your setting. Brainstorm with your partner for creative ideas.

☐ Discuss involving others. Brainstorm with your partner and develop a plan for involving others as you think best fits your setting.

☐ Write your specific feedback about these teaching materials and send it to the developers.*

*Social Effectiveness Training, P.O. Box 6664, Reno, Nev. 89513.

Chapter 3

Establishing Standards for Social Behavior

Importance of Confidence

One of the most important components of successful "instructor behavior" is an attitude of confidence. With confidence, you as an instructor can avoid hesitations that rob credibility or create "loop-holes" that may be tested by children. If you have confidence, you will inspire confidence in children and create a nonthreatening, relaxed atmosphere for yourself and the children. Initial attempts with new skills are always awkward, and children need to feel secure enough to try new behaviors or to exhibit existing problematic behaviors. Therefore the atmosphere you create for their learning is very important.

You can achieve confidence by having a thorough familiarity with the content and scripts in the curriculum, as well as by becoming certain about personal expectations and standards for social behavior and communicating them clearly to the children. If your behavioral expectations are clear in any situation, you will be more spontaneous, and you will be ready to respond quickly and smoothly.

This chapter is designed to help you develop clarity about social behavior expectations. After reading this chapter and completing the activities included in it, you should (1) be familiar with the 17 core skills, (2) be prepared to carefully observe children in interactional settings and identify specific behavioral goals, and (3) be able to clearly articulate your own standards.

Curriculum

The curriculum provides specific behavioral components for skills identified in the program. These skills were suggested by consumers: parents, teachers, principals, counselors, children, and others (Jackson, 1978). The positive response to children after training suggests that using these particular skills can have a powerful influence on the way children are perceived. The curriculum offers a set of "core" standards. You may wish to adopt them in their entirety or incorporate them in a set of standards you devise. With either approach, the skills will provide you with a model of how social behavior may be defined and presented as an explicit curriculum.

In the following list you will find the social skills covered in the curriculum. Please note that each skill has a limited number of very specific behavioral components which define that skill for the child. All incorporate the requirements for a "good attitude" (pleasant face, pleasant voice, and eye contact). These skills and their components are taken directly from the corresponding skill lessons in *Skill Lessons and Activities*.

Core Social Skills

Skill 1: **Introducing**
To introduce yourself to someone, you:
- Use a pleasant face and voice.
- Look at the person.
- Tell the person your name.
- Ask for the person's name.

To introduce two people who don't know each other, you:
- Use a pleasant face and voice.
- Look at each person.
- Tell each person the other's name.

Skill 2: **Following Directions**
To follow directions, you:
- Use a pleasant face and voice.
- Look at the person giving the directions.

- Say "OK."
- Start to do what was asked right away.
- Do it satisfactorily.

Skill 3: **Giving and Receiving Positive Feedback**
To give Positive Feedback, you:
- Use a pleasant face and voice.
- Look at the person.
- Tell exactly what you like about what the person did.
- Tell the person right after it was done.

To receive Positive Feedback, you:
- Use a pleasant face and voice.
- Look at the person.
- Acknowledge the feedback by saying, "Thanks" or, "You're welcome."

Skill 4: **Sending an "I'm Interested" Message**
To send an "I'm interested" message, you:
- Use a pleasant face.
- Look at the person.
- Keep your hands and body still.

Skill 5: **Sending an Ignoring Message**
To send an ignoring message, you:
- Keep a pleasant face.
- Look away or walk away from the person.
- Keep a quiet mouth.
- Pretend you're not listening.

Skill 6: **Interrupting a Conversation**
To interrupt the right way, you:
- Use a pleasant face and voice.
- Wait for a pause in the conversation.
- Say "Excuse me."
- Look directly at the person.
- Then talk.

Skill 7: **Joining a Conversation**
To join a conversation, you:
- Use a pleasant face and voice.
- Look at the person.
- Wait for a pause.
- Say something on the topic.

Skill 8: **Starting a Conversation and Keeping It Going**
To start a conversation and keep it going, you:
- Use a pleasant face and voice.
- Look at the person.
- Ask questions about the other person.
- Tell about yourself.

Skill 9: **Sharing**
To share, you:
- Use a pleasant face and voice.
- Divide up something there's not much of, so others can also have some (if appropriate).
- Take turns (if appropriate).

Skill 10: **Offering to Help**
To offer to help, you:
- Use a pleasant face and voice.
- Notice something that you can do for someone.
- Ask if you can help.
- If that person says "yes," then you do it.

Skill 11: **Compromising**
To compromise, you:
- Use a pleasant face and voice.
- Think of a way both people can get something that they want.
- Suggest it.

Skill 12: **Asking for Clear Directions**
To ask for clear directions, you:
- Use a pleasant face and voice.
- Look at the person.
- Ask for more information.
- Repeat the directions to the person.

Skill 13: **Problem Solving**
To solve a problem, you:
- Take a deep breath to get a calm body and good attitude.
- Think of at least three different things you can do.
- Pick the best one for you.
- Try that one first.

Skill 14: **Using Positive Consequences**
To reward someone, you:
- Use a pleasant face and voice.
- Do something nice for the person.

  For example, you could do the person a favor, thank the person, give the person a hug, or share something.

Skill 15: **Giving and Receiving a Suggestion for Improvement**
To give a suggestion for improvement, you:
- Use a pleasant face and voice.
- Say something nice on the topic.
- Make the suggestion.
- Thank the person for listening.*

To receive a suggestion for improvement, you:
- Use a pleasant face and voice.
- Listen to the suggestion.
- Make no excuses.
- Thank the person for the suggestion.

Skill 16: **Handling Name-Calling and Teasing**
To handle name-calling and teasing, you:
- Keep a pleasant face.
- Take a deep breath to get calm.
- Look away, or walk away if you can.
- Use positive self-talk (say to self, "I am calm," etc.).

Skill 17: **Saying "No" to Stay Out of Trouble**
To say "no," you:
- Use a pleasant face and voice.
- Take a deep breath to get calm.
- Look at the person.
- Keep saying "no."
- Suggest something else to do.

If suggesting something else doesn't work, you:
- Ignore and walk away.

*When using with young or low-functioning children, substitute these components: "I like the way you. . .," "It might be better if you . . .," and "Thanks for listening."

12

Recognizing Individual Needs

A vital process for making individual priorities clear for both the child and you as teacher is that of selecting and defining target behaviors. The same behavior may mean different things within the context of the individual needs of different children. Part of your success in dealing with children will depend on your ability to judge the situation clearly and accurately and establish priorities. In working with a group of children, you will constantly have to make decisions about which behavior to attend to and what to let slide. For example, there may be times when too many behaviors needing your attention are occurring at one time. At that point how do you decide whether to work on strengthening Joyce's hand-raising or decreasing Cathy's talking out? It all depends on the children and your understanding of their social skills strengths and weaknesses. If Joyce is extremely withdrawn and this is her first time to volunteer, your response might be different from the one you would make if volunteering were not a severe problem for Joyce but talking out were for Cathy.

Selecting Target Behaviors

Each child's individual target behaviors are based on the problems identified by you, and others who see the child, including classroom teachers, parents, and counselors. If possible, you as the instructor should arrange a meeting with the parents to discuss the presenting problems and mutually select the target behaviors. In addition, other professionals in contact with the child might be consulted for input. Through discussion of the child's behavior, you can identify problem areas and articulate the child's unique goals. State these as the desired behaviors.

The following is a list of the target behaviors we used most commonly. Notice that most of them are defined by suggested behavioral components. Those not defined by behavioral components are actual core skills that have already been defined. Notice, too, that target behaviors are stated positively, i.e., what the child *will* do rather than what she is *not* to do.

Keep this list in mind as you do Activity 2.

Common Target Behaviors

I have a good attitude:
    Use a pleasant face and voice.
    Look at the person.

I keep my hands to myself:
    Keep hands (and feet) off others.
    Keep hands (and feet) off others' belongings.

I ask, not tell:
    Use a pleasant face and voice.
    Use please and thank you.
    Ask, using a question.
    Accept "no" as an answer.

I cooperate with others:
    Use a pleasant face and voice.
    Offer to help.
    Help when asked.
    Follow directions.

I volunteer:
    Use a pleasant face and voice.
    Raise hand with a quiet mouth.
    Keep a still body.
    Give on-topic answers.

I take responsibility for myself (addresses blaming, lying, and excuse-making behaviors):
    Use a pleasant face and voice.

Answer questions honestly.
    Make no excuses.
    Accept consequences with a good attitude.

I take responsibility *just* for myself (addresses tattling, gossiping, and bossing others):
    Use a pleasant face and voice.
    Improve own behavior.
    Let others improve their own behavior.
    Talk about self.

I join in with others:
    Use a pleasant face and voice.
    Use please and thank you.
    Ask others if you can join them.
    Accept "no" as an answer.

I let others decide:
    Use a pleasant face and voice.
    Wait or ask for others to make suggestions.
    Make suggestions, using a question.
    Accept "no" as an answer.

I let others talk:
    Use a pleasant face and voice.
    Look at the person.
    Ask questions to show interest.
    Pause when talking so that others may talk as much as you do.

I let others do fun things:
    Use a pleasant face and voice.
    Let others take turns or be first.

I have a calm body:
    Keep a pleasant face and quiet voice.
    Keep a still and relaxed body.

I use an inside voice:
    Keep a pleasant and quiet voice when inside an enclosed area (e.g., a room, car, or building).

I use short, on-topic answers:
    Use a pleasant face and voice.

Look at the other person(s).
Give a short answer about the same thing others are discussing.

I follow directions (see skill).

I am a good listener (see Sending an "I'm Interested" Message).

I problem solve (see skill).

I say nice things to others (see Giving and Receiving Positive Feedback).

Activity 2. Choosing Target Behaviors

This activity provides the type of background information from which you might initially choose target behaviors for the child. Read the following excerpt from a parent's initial interview with a program instructor. There is valuable information both in what the mother says and in what she implies. However, for the purpose of this exercise, resist the temptation to analyze the mother; focus instead on the child's specific areas of need. Decide on four target behaviors for this child and write them in the spaces provided. Check your answers against those suggested in Appendix B.

Mother:

I just don't know what to do about my son, Jason. He's so nasty and belligerent whenever I tell him to do anything. I just can't relate to him anymore. And it seems like nobody else can either. He doesn't seem to have any friends. When he tries to play with other children, it always ends with an argument, with the other child telling Jason he's mean and always wants things his way. Then Jason just seems to get meaner. He acts as if he doesn't care about anything. His grades are dropping. I know he can do good work, but he just doesn't bother. Sometimes he doesn't even bring his books home, and I know he must have homework. He's so disorganized – or maybe he's just looking for an easy out. I just don't know what to do with him.

Write Jason's target behaviors in the spaces below:

1. _____

2. _____

3. _____

4. _____

Defining Target Behaviors

Target behaviors should be defined very specifically with no more than four behavioral components each and then stated in a positive and simple way so the child will understand. For example, a child whose identified problem is "bossiness" with his peers might be learning to "ask, not tell," or "let others decide." The target behavior "ask, not tell," could have the following behavioral components: use a pleasant face and voice; use please and thank you; ask, using a question; accept "no" as an answer.

Activity 3. Defining Target Behaviors

Complete the Target Behavior Worksheet (on the following page), defining Jason's target behaviors (selected in Activity 2). You might want to use the worksheet with all or some of the children in your setting to establish target behaviors. See Appendix B for some suggested answers regarding Jason.

Once you select and define three to five target behaviors for each child, it is important to introduce and support those behaviors in ways which will remind the child to work on them. In order for the child to remember her target behaviors so that she can practice them, always state them in the same way, making sure that the behavioral components are not altered. As you introduce the child's target behaviors to her, model the behavioral components. The Target Behavior Worksheet, which follows, may be used to discuss the breakdown of the child's behaviors with her. The child must be aware of what her target behaviors are, and she must be able to physically demonstrate the behavioral components. Encourage the child to practice the target behaviors in her interactions with others.

If you begin the group using target behaviors suggested by others (parents, teachers, etc.), you may wish to revise them somewhat after observing the child in your setting. Children's behavior sometimes changes quite markedly in different settings. They may display entirely different problem behaviors or different versions of those initially anticipated. For instance, a child whose physical fighting and name-calling is a problem at home may display only a failure to cooperate in the program setting. Except for considerations such as these, you should delete a target behavior or replace it with a new one *only* after the child can consistently use it in everyday interactions. As the child acquires new skills, you can help to maintain their use through descriptive praise and approval.

Establishing Your Own Standards

Once you are familiar with the core skills, you should carefully examine your own ideas about social behavior to determine whether you wish to adopt the curriculum or adapt it to fit your needs. The process of deciding what behaviors and components are desirable involves *value judgments* that may be influenced by the cultural values and styles of your setting. Any decisions about goals for children should be directed at providing for the child's social survival in his environment.

Once you have described and are familiar with *your* set of standards (including core skills you've chosen), you will have created the behavioral reference with which to assess interactional situations. This will allow you, for the most part, to judge a situation immediately and respond fairly, in a manner which will provide for a positive learning experience for the child or children involved.

As you decide what your expectations are, however, be sure that you articulate them with clarity and specificity. Activity 4, on page 17, is designed to give you practice in developing your own specific definitions of social behavior for some typical situations.

Target Behavior Worksheet

I, _____, agree to work on improving my social skills by doing the following things:

1. _____

which means I: _____,

_____,

_____, and

_____.

2. _____

which means I: _____,

_____,

_____, and

_____.

3. _____

which means I: _____,

_____,

_____, and

_____.

4. _____

which means I: _____,

_____,

_____, and

_____.

Activity 4. Defining Behaviors and Establishing Standards

This exercise will give you practice in developing skill definitions with specific behavioral components that fit *your* standards for social behavior.

If a child typically asks for things in a bossy or demanding way, his target behavior might be "asking nicely." Complete the following definition for "asking nicely." Check your answers against suggested ones in Appendix B.

Asking Nicely

To ask nicely, you:

1. _____
2. _____
3. _____
4. _____

Complete the following definitions for "lining up," "getting a drink," and "participating in a group discussion." Check your answers against suggested ones in Appendix B.

Lining Up

To line up, you:

1. _____
2. _____
3. _____
4. _____

Getting a Drink

To get a drink in this class, you:

1. _____
2. _____
3. _____
4. _____

Participating in a Group Discussion

To participate in a group discussion, you:

1. _____
2. _____
3. _____
4. _____

Establishing Rules

Establishing a list of rules for your program is another important way to define expectations for behavior. You should display and discuss these rules with the children during the first group meeting and then permanently post them for quick reference. It is extremely important that you and the children are clear about what behaviors are appropriate. A rule board might look like the following example.

```
                 Rules
        1.  I follow directions.
        2.  I keep my hands to myself.
        3.  I keep a good attitude.
        4.  I look at the speaker.
        5.  I raise my hand with a
            quiet mouth.
```

Analyzing Situations

When you are confident about your expectations and standards for social behavior, you can analyze and categorize a child's behavior in each situation as "correct" or "needing improvement." Only when you can do this accurately can you apply the Teaching Strategies to ensure that no learning opportunities are lost.

Most situations in which children are behaving, no matter how inappropriately, include at least some minor appropriate behaviors. Effective application of the Teaching Strategies will depend on your ability to determine what part of the behavior is already correct and what part of it needs to improve. Activity 5, which follows, will give you some practice in analyzing some typical situations.

Activity 5. Analyzing Situations

Read the situation and for the italicized character determine what part of the behavior is correct (if any), what part of the behavior is incorrect, and what the complete correct behavior would look like. To do this, you will need to be aware of your own expectations and standards for appropriate social behavior. Appendix B includes some suggested answers based on the standards in the curriculum.

Example:

Situation:
Three children are playing basketball; one *child* is hogging the ball.

A correct behavior here is: child is playing with others.

The incorrect behavior here is: child is hogging the ball.

The complete correct behavior here would be: child shares or takes turns.

Situation:
You are in a group setting. One *child* is picking up objects off the floor and playing with them.

A correct behavior here is: _____.

The incorrect behavior here is: _____.

The complete correct behavior here would be: _____.

Situation:

During the lesson *one of the children* makes noises such as obtrusive throat clearing, singing, and belching.

A correct behavior here is: _____.

The incorrect behavior here is: _____.

The complete correct behavior here would be: _____.

Situation:

You give one child directions to set up the snack. Another *child* who is working on bossiness-type behaviors says, "Oh, I'll do it Charles, I'll do it with you, let me help!"

A correct behavior here is: _____.

The incorrect behavior here is: _____.

The complete correct behavior here would be: _____.

Situation:

Two children are playing together, and one *child* impatiently says to the other in a harsh tone of voice, "It's your turn now!"

A correct behavior here is: _____.

The incorrect behavior here is: _____.

The complete correct behavior here would be: _____.

Situation:

A child is giving Positive Feedback to another child. The *child* giving the feedback tells the other one a specific event that was positive, uses a pleasant tone of voice, but has a grouchy-looking face.

A correct behavior here is: _____.

The incorrect behavior here is: _____.

The complete correct behavior here would be: _____.

Situation:

You are giving instructions for the children to clean up paints after activity time and go to the circle. One *child* says, in a nice voice, "In a minute."

A correct behavior here is: _____.

The incorrect behavior here is: _____.

The complete correct behavior here would be: _____.

Situation:

You are giving directions to a *child* who responds by slamming things around and saying, "Oh, all right!"
When you say to the child, "It would be better if you followed my directions with a good attitude," the child says, "But I was, I had a good attitude, I did what you said!"

A correct behavior here is: _____.

The incorrect behavior here is: _____.

The complete correct behavior here would be: _____.

Situation:

On the playground a really withdrawn *child* is standing on the fringes watching other children play.

A correct behavior here is: _____.

The incorrect behavior here is: _____.

The complete correct behavior here would be: _____.

Situation:

In the group you prompt for Positive Feedback following a role play. One *child* volunteers appropriately, you call on him, and he says, "I hiked to the top of a mountain last night."

A correct behavior here is: _____.

The incorrect behavior here is: _____.

The complete correct behavior here would be: _____.

Situation:

During game time you prompt the children to go over and choose a game and play together. One *child* turns to you and says, "I want to play with you, Teacher."

A correct behavior here is: _____.

The incorrect behavior here is: _____.

The complete correct behavior here would be: _____.

Situation:

The group is preparing for a circle time. Children are sitting in the circle quietly, and one *child* approaches you and sits on your lap.

A correct behavior here is: _____.

The incorrect behavior here is: _____.

The complete correct behavior here would be: _____.

Situation:

It is snack time, and the children are having a conversation. One *child* who is sitting in the middle of the group is watching the other children, nodding her head, but not saying anything.

A correct behavior here is: _____.

The incorrect behavior here is: _____.

The complete correct behavior here would be: _____.

Chapter 4

Using the Five Teaching Strategies and Other Techniques

This chapter is designed to train you to use the five Teaching Strategies: Positive Feedback, Ignore-Attend-Praise, the Teaching Interaction, Direct Prompt, and Sit and Watch. Guidelines for using the Teaching Strategies provide you with a means for judging which strategy to use. In addition, the chapter describes other teaching techniques involving getting the children "ready," making transitions run smoothly, rehearsing for high-risk settings, making privileges contingent, teaching children to "take responsibility," teaching problem solving, using a verbal prompting sequence, using physical prompting, and using coaching.

The Five Teaching Strategies

The technology for using ongoing events, whatever they are, as the vehicle for teaching and supporting social behaviors is the component of the program that we have considered the most valuable. The five Teaching Strategies provide that technology.

The recurring message from program users is that the Teaching Strategies make teaching easier and more rewarding. The strategies provide options for handling difficult situations. Employing the Teaching Strategies will give you the opportunity to be a facilitator, supporter, and teacher, rather than a watch dog or police officer. You can maintain a positive identity for yourself while helping the children experience success in learning. You will be better equipped to resolve tense situations positively so that everyone involved feels better.

The purpose of the Teaching Strategies is to elicit or strengthen appropriate behaviors so that the child can experience success and social approval. When the Teaching Strategies are used as outlined, there is no need for negative interactions with the child. Appropriate behavior is continually praised while behavior that needs improvement is interrupted positively so that the child may practice more appropriate behavior, experience success, and then receive approval.

All of the Teaching Strategies may be included under one title, "incidental teaching." Incidental teaching refers to the use of an ongoing event as the subject matter for teaching a concept or skill. Nearly all of the child's behavior may be used by you as the basis for teaching social skills.

That's the good news. The not-so-good news is that the Teaching Strategies are the hardest part of the program to learn. They require a style of interacting which may be awkward to you at first. Don't be surprised if this style of interaction does not seem to come naturally. Most people learning the strategies experience some frustration at first, but they find that they can master them by role playing diligently and then applying them to real-life situations.

This chapter is designed not only to establish the Teaching Strategies in your skill repertoire but also to demonstrate how to select a strategy for a given situation. Suggestions and cautions about usage are included with the presentation of each. Guidelines for judging which strategy is most appropriate for a particular situation are provided at the end of the Teaching Strategies section of this chapter.

Learning the Teaching Strategies

This chapter introduces each strategy, defines it in terms of its components, and discusses how it is used. To facilitate your learning and applying each strategy, the chapter also provides a set of activities. You will familiarize yourself with the strategies by completing activities that include memorizing the components, describing how the components are used in right-way vignettes, and analyzing vignettes in a process of discrimination training. Then, most importantly, you will use the skills in activities that provide you with opportunities to role play and practice in a real-life setting. Blank Evaluation Checksheets are provided with the additional vignettes for role playing each Teaching Strategy with your partner. You will need to make photocopies of the Evaluation Checksheets for you and your partner to use in evaluating your performances and giving each other feedback in your training meetings.

The Training Checksheet and Agendas for Meetings (both in Chapter 2) indicate the suggested method and sequence for using all these activities.

Positive Feedback

Description

Positive Feedback must be positive, specific, immediate, and true. It is ideally the final outcome of all interactions with the children, since their behavior should always culminate in the successful use of the skill. Positive Feedback serves two very important functions. It is, in most cases, a strong motivator (a social reinforcer). That is, it provides a positive social consequence and therefore may increase the likelihood of future occurrences of the desirable behavior. (Whether or not a child is "reinforced" by a given consequence is a highly individual matter, and you should not assume that praise is a reinforcer for all children. However, the use of contingent social praise has been successful with most children in the program.) Positive Feedback is also a very important instructional tool. Since you as teacher name exactly what behavior was correct and desirable, the child knows exactly what behavior to repeat.

Whenever you use Positive Feedback, be sure you are making it specific to the *behavior*, not the *child*. That is, say, "You are really looking up here and listening now," not "You are a good listener," or "That was thoughtful; you shared your juice," instead of "You really are thoughtful." The purpose of Positive Feedback is to help children strengthen behaviors which will make successful interactions with others more likely. Your purpose is not to judge the child's worth as a person; positive or negative judgments about personality can have a damaging effect, communicating "You are only good as long as you are acting the way I want you to."

Use

Positive Feedback should be used *whenever* behavior to be strengthened or maintained occurs. An observant teacher will find something to praise in the children's behavior in almost all situations. Typically, skilled instructors of this program use Positive Feedback at a rate of about four times per minute.

Activity 6. Memorizing the Components

Positive Feedback is:
1. *Positive.*
2. *Specific.*
3. *Immediate.*
4. *True.*

Activity 7. Right-Way Vignette for Positive Feedback

When used correctly, the strategy should look like this:

In the group children are getting ready for snack time. A child is pouring juice into a cup, but it slides. Another child says, "Here, let me help you," and holds the cup.

Teacher:
Billy, that's really neat. You just cooperated with Shawn so that he could pour the juice.

Describe how the components of Positive Feedback were correctly used in this example.

Activity 8. Discrimination Training for Positive Feedback

Read the following vignettes. Notice if each component is used correctly. Circle *Yes* if the component was done completely and correctly. Use the lines to write exactly what made it correct. Circle *No* if all or parts of the component were incorrect or incomplete. Use the lines to describe what could have happened to make it correct. Check your answers for each vignette against those in Appendix B before going to the next vignette.

The setting for these vignettes is as follows:

Children are getting ready for snack time. One child is pouring juice into a cup, but it slides. Another child says, "Here, let me help you," and holds the cup.

Vignette 1

Teacher:
Good work, boys.

1. Teacher made a statement that was *positive*.   Yes   No

_____

_____

_____

2. Teacher made a statement that was *specific*.   Yes   No

_____

_____

_____

3. Teacher made the statement *immediately after* the appropriate behavior.   Yes   No

_____

_____

_____

4. Teacher made a statement that was *true*.   Yes   No

_____

_____

_____

Vignette 2

Teacher:
Wow, what a great guy you are, Billy.

1. Teacher made a statement that was *positive*.   Yes   No

_____

_____

_____

2. Teacher made a statement that was *specific*.   Yes   No

_____

_____

_____

3. Teacher made the statement *immediately after* the   Yes   No
   appropriate behavior.

_____

_____

_____

4. Teacher made a statement that was *true*.   Yes   No

_____

_____

_____

Vignette 3

Teacher:
Thanks, Billy, for helping Shawn. I didn't really feel like cleaning up the mess.

1. Teacher made a statement that was *positive*.   Yes   No

_____

_____

_____

2. Teacher made a statement that was *specific*.   Yes   No

_____

_____

_____

3. Teacher made the statement *immediately after* the   Yes   No
   appropriate behavior.

_____

_____

_____

4. Teacher made a statement that was *true*.   Yes   No

_____

_____

_____

Activity 9. Vignettes for Role Playing Positive Feedback

Role play the following vignettes with your partner, alternating the teacher and child parts. Use the Evaluation Checksheet which follows.

A child whose target behavior is bossiness asks another child to "please pass the juice."

A youngster's target behavior is on-topic remarks. After a role play, he volunteers and says, "You were looking right at the speaker."

A shy child raises his hand.

At snack time a child shows interest in another by asking, "What are you going to do tonight, Jim?"

You ask a child to bring the garbage can over, and she says, "Sure," and immediately does it.

A child walks up to another child outside and asks him if he'd like to play ball.

There aren't enough apples at snack time, so one child offers another child half of hers.

You ask a child to clean up his game. He usually whines and complains, but this time he answers, "Sure," and cleans up right away with a good attitude.

One youngster who tends to lie and tell imaginative stories to impress others joins into a conversation by telling about something that's believable.

A child has really been paying attention to you by keeping his body still and looking right at you.

A child who usually talks on and on about herself lets a classmate talk while she listens quietly.

A group of children have finished their work early and are quietly playing a game together.

A group of children are playing basketball together; one child compliments someone on a shot.

At snack time a child joins an ongoing conversation without interrupting and talks on the subject.

Evaluation Checksheet: Positive Feedback

Instructions:

Observe your partner role play. Watch for the correct use of each component. Circle *Yes* if the component was done completely and correctly. Use the lines to write exactly what made it correct. Circle *No* if all or parts of the component were incorrect or incomplete. Describe what could have happened to make it correct.

1. Teacher made a statement that was *positive*.   Yes   No

_____

_____

_____

2. Teacher made a statement that was *specific*.   Yes   No

_____

_____

_____

3. Teacher made the statement *immediately after* the   Yes   No
   appropriate behavior.

_____

_____

_____

4. Teacher made a statement that was *true*.   Yes   No

_____

_____

_____

Activity 10. Homework for Positive Feedback

Complete the following Homework exercise in a real setting. Compare your use of the strategy with the components listed in Activity 6.

Within the next day or so, find five situations in which you can use Positive Feedback. In the spaces provided, specifically describe each situation and exactly what you said in using Positive Feedback.

Situation 1: _____

_____

    What I said: _____

_____

Situation 2: _____

_____

    What I said: _____

_____

Situation 3: _____

_____

    What I said: _____

_____

Situation 4: _____

_____

    What I said: _____

_____

Situation 5: _____

_____

    What I said: _____

_____

Ignore-Attend-Praise

Description

The Ignore-Attend-Praise sequence serves two purposes. It reinforces one child who is behaving appropriately while prompting another child who is behaving inappropriately. Instead of attending to a child behaving inappropriately, you look for a child who is displaying the desired behavior and praise the child in such a way that the child behaving inappropriately can hear.

Use

The Ignore-Attend-Praise sequence is an extremely useful tool in teaching the program. Because it focuses only on positive behaviors, it helps to keep the overall tone of the group positive. It is especially useful with "attention-getting" misbehaviors since there is no attention as a payoff for that behavior.

Activity 11. Memorizing the Components

To use Ignore-Attend-Praise:

1. *Ignore* the child behaving inappropriately.

2. *Attend* to and praise the child behaving appropriately. This serves to maintain the behavior and prompt the child who is behaving inappropriately.

3. When the child who is misbehaving begins to behave appropriately, attend to and *praise* the child.

Activity 12. Right-Way Vignette for Ignore-Attend-Praise

When used correctly, the strategy should look like this:

Johnny and Susie have been asked to clean up the snack table. Johnny has begun the task, but Susie is just watching.

Teacher:
Johnny, you're following my directions really well. You remembered to get up and begin cleaning up right away, and with a good attitude, too.

(Susie hears teacher praise Johnny and begins to help.)

Teacher:
Susie, thanks for helping to clean up like I asked you to. You are really cooperating.

Describe how the components of Ignore-Attend-Praise were used correctly in this example.

Activity 13. Discrimination Training for Ignore-Attend-Praise

Read the following vignettes. Notice if each component is used correctly. Circle *Yes* if the component was done completely and correctly. Use the lines to write exactly what made it correct. Circle *No* if all or parts of the component were incorrect or incomplete. Use the lines to describe what could have happened to make it correct. Check your answers for each vignette against those in Appendix B before going to the next vignette.

The setting for these vignettes is as follows:
Johnny and Susie have been asked to clean up the snack table. Johnny has begun the task, but Susie is just watching.

Vignette 1

Teacher:
Johnny, you are following my directions really well. Susie, you need to help out also.

Child:
OK.

Teacher:
Thanks for beginning to cooperate.

1. Teacher *ignored* the child behaving inappropriately.   Yes   No

_____

_____

2. Teacher *attended* to and praised the child behaving appropriately.   Yes   No

_____

_____

3. Teacher *praised* the child when the behavior became appropriate.   Yes   No

_____

_____

_____

Vignette 2

Teacher:
Johnny, you are really helping out by following my directions right away.

(Susie hears teacher praise Johnny and begins to help.)

Teacher:
Well, it's about time you started to help out; you would have gotten the job finished sooner if you had started right away.

1. Teacher *ignored* the child behaving inappropriately.   Yes   No

_____

_____

_____

2. Teacher *attended* to and praised the child behaving appropriately.   Yes   No

_____

_____

3. Teacher *praised* the child when the behavior became appropriate.   Yes   No

_____

_____

Vignette 3

Teacher:
Susie, you should be following my directions.

(Susie begins to clean up.)

Teacher:
That's better.

1. Teacher *ignored* the child behaving inappropriately.   Yes   No

_____

_____

2. Teacher *attended* to and praised the child behaving appropriately.   Yes   No

_____

_____

3. Teacher *praised* the child when the behavior became appropriate.   Yes   No

_____

_____

_____

Activity 14. Vignettes for Role Playing Ignore-Attend-Praise

Role play the following vignettes with your partner, alternating the teacher and child parts. A third person (or an imaginary child) will be needed. Use the Evaluation Checksheet which follows.

Mike is setting up a board game while his partner, Sam, watches.

You have asked the group to set the table for snack time. Johnny and Susie are pouring juice while Tim and Ann are talking about a movie.

During a group "circle time" you notice that Mike, Johnny, and Ann are looking at the speaker, but Sam and Tim are not.

On the playground Tim is complying with playground rules while Johnny is kicking sand.

You have asked everyone to line up at the door to go out to the playground. Tim and Sam line up right away, but Johnny, Susie, Ann, and Mike remain at the snack table.

You have asked Tim and Susie to help Ann carry some games to the closet. Tim does not respond, but Susie gets up to help.

At snack time you have organized a group discussion. Everyone except Mike is adding to the conversation.

During relaxation time all children except Mike are very carefully trying the exercises.

While two children are role playing, Mike and Ann are listening, but Tim is looking out the window.

When you are giving the instructions for an activity, only Ann is sitting still *and* looking at you.

Out on the playground Mike, Joe, and Ann are playing nicely with each other; Steve is standing against a wall, frowning.

A group of children are playing basketball together; Billy misses his shot; Ann says, "Good try," and John says, "I knew you couldn't make that one."

Evaluation Checksheet: Ignore-Attend-Praise

Instructions:

Observe your partner role play. Watch for the correct use of each component. Circle *Yes* if the component was done completely and correctly. Use the lines to write exactly what made it correct. Circle *No* if all or parts of the component were incorrect or incomplete. Describe what could have happened to make it correct.

1. Teacher *ignored* the child behaving inappropriately.   Yes   No

_____

_____

_____

2. Teacher *attended* to and praised the child behaving appropriately.   Yes   No

_____

_____

_____

3. Teacher *praised* the child when the behavior became appropriate.   Yes   No

_____

_____

_____

Activity 15. Homework for Ignore-Attend-Praise

Complete the following Homework exercise in a real setting. Compare your use of the strategy with the components listed in Activity 11.

Within the next day or so, find five situations in which you can use Ignore-Attend-Praise. In the spaces provided, specifically describe each situation and exactly what you said in using Ignore-Attend-Praise.

Situation 1: _____

_____

What I said: _____

_____

Situation 2: _____

_____

What I said: _____

_____

Situation 3: _____

_____

What I said: _____

_____

Situation 4: _____

_____

What I said: _____

_____

Situation 5: _____

_____

What I said: _____

_____

Teaching Interaction

Description

The Teaching Interaction is a positive intervention in a situation in which improvement is needed in an aspect of a child's social behavior. The Teaching Interaction . may be used to teach a new skill, strengthen weak use of a skill, or deal with an inappropriate occurrence. Basically, you as teacher interrupt the inappropriate behavior in a positive way, ask the child to suggest an alternative behavior (modeling or verbalizing this yourself, if the child can't), and ask the child to practice the appropriate behavior. The practice component provides for some immediate success in a nonthreatening atmosphere. Of course, you support *any* improvement in the behavior with praise. Giving the child homework completes the interaction.

Use

The Teaching Interaction described in the program is a shortened and simplified version of a procedure developed by the staff that originated the "Teaching Family Model" (Maloney, Phillips, Fixsen, & Wolf, 1975; Phillips, Phillips, Fixsen, & Wolf, 1974). The Teaching Interaction is basically an interpersonal problem-solving technique.

Since the Teaching Interaction starts with a positive statement, the listener is more receptive. Having the child provide or repeat the suggestion for improvement emphasizes the appropriate behavior. The practice section is the most important part of the Teaching Interaction; it ensures that the appropriate behavior is practiced in the same real-life context in which the inappropriate behavior just occurred. Just as Positive Feedback utilizes appropriate occurrences of behavior to teach social skills, the Teaching Interaction utilizes inappropriate occurrences of behavior to teach social skills. Thus, a negative interaction does not end as such, but rather is used to teach a more effective, positive approach in that situation. You acknowledge a child's successful practice of the desired skill with Positive Feedback. In using Positive Feedback, you support the child's efforts and restate the appropriate behavioral components.

The Teaching Interaction is best used in situations in which you may intervene with one or two children and focus energy on those children. It is especially useful in settings such as snack time, activity time, free play, or game time. Appropriate use during a lesson would likely be to refine a skill being role played or a specific skill targeted for a child. Examples of appropriate occasions for the Teaching Interaction during a lesson might include (1) when a child has just role played a skill, using all components except one – for instance, eye-contact – or (2) when a child uses the third person instead of the second in giving feedback.

Activity 16. Memorizing the Components

To use the Teaching Interaction:

1. Interrupt the inappropriate behavior by *saying something positive* that is related to the situation.

2. Ask the child for an *alternative way of behaving*. If the child doesn't know, you *verbalize* or *model* one and have the child repeat it.

3. Ask the child to *practice* the appropriate behavior.

4. Give the child *positive feedback* for *any* improvement.

5. Give the child *homework*.

Activity 17. Right-Way Vignette for the Teaching Interaction

When used correctly, the strategy should look like this:

The yard-duty teacher is talking to a child on the playground. Another child, who is shy, approaches them and interrupts.

Child:
Teacher, teacher, I just made two baskets in our game!

Teacher:
I'm really glad that you want to tell me something about yourself! How could you do that without interrupting?

Child:
I could wait for you to stop talking.

Teacher:
Right, you could wait for a pause in our conversation. Let's practice that right now. Susie and I are going to continue to talk about soccer, and you will wait for a pause and then tell me about your baskets.

(The teacher and Susie talk; the child waits for a pause.)

Child:
Teacher, I just made two baskets in our basketball game.

Teacher:
Good for you. That time you waited for a pause. And thanks for practicing that with such a good attitude! The next time you want to tell someone something, remember to wait for a pause in the conversation like you did just now.

(The conversation about baskets resumes.)

Describe how the components of the Teaching Interaction were correctly used in this example.

Activity 18. Discrimination Training for the Teaching Interaction

Read the following vignettes. Notice if each component is used correctly. Circle *Yes* if the component was done completely and correctly. Use the lines to write exactly what made it correct. Circle *No* if all or parts of the component were incorrect or incomplete. Use the lines to describe what could have happened to make it correct. Check your answers for each vignette against those in Appendix B before going to the next vignette.

The setting for these vignettes is as follows:

The yard-duty teacher is talking to a child on the playground. Another child, who is withdrawn, approaches them and interrupts.

Vignette 1

Teacher:
Johnny, it's really nice that you want to talk to us. It might be nicer if you did it without interrupting. Please do that from now on. OK?

Child:
OK.

1. Teacher stopped the interaction by *saying something positive* that was related to the situation.   Yes   No

_____

_____

_____

2. Teacher asked the child for an *alternative way of behaving*. If the child didn't know, the teacher *verbalized* or *modeled* one and had the child repeat it.   Yes   No

_____

_____

_____

3. Teacher asked the child to *practice* the appropriate behavior.   Yes   No

_____

_____

_____

4. Teacher gave the child *Positive Feedback* for *any* improvement.   Yes   No

_____

_____

_____

5. Teacher gave the child *homework*.   Yes   No

_____

_____

_____

Vignette 2

Teacher:
Johnny, it would be better if you didn't interrupt. How could you do that?

Child:
While you are talking, I could wait for a pause.

Teacher:
That's a really good idea. Susie and I are going to continue to talk, and you can show me how you would do that.

(The teacher and Susie talk; the child waits for a pause.)

Child:
Teacher, I just made two baskets in our basketball game.

Teacher:
What a nice way to join our conversation! And thanks for practicing that with a good attitude. The next time you want to interrupt a conversation, I want you to try to remember to wait for a pause.

1. Teacher stopped the interaction by *saying something positive*   Yes   No
   that was related to the situation.

_____

_____

_____

2. Teacher asked the child for an *alternative way of behaving*. If the   Yes   No
   child didn't know, the teacher *verbalized* or *modeled* one and had
   the child repeat it.

_____

_____

_____

3. Teacher asked the child to *practice* the appropriate behavior.   Yes   No

_____

_____

_____

4. Teacher gave the child *Positive Feedback* for *any* improvement.   Yes   No

_____

_____

_____

5. Teacher gave the child *homework*.   Yes   No

_____

_____

_____

Vignette 3

Teacher:
Johnny, it's really nice that you want to tell me something about yourself. And it might even be nicer if you didn't interrupt. How could you do that?

Child:
I could wait for you to stop talking.

Teacher:
What a nice idea.

1. Teacher stopped the interaction by *saying something positive* that was related to the situation.   Yes   No

_____

_____

_____

2. Teacher asked the child for an *alternative way of behaving*. If the child didn't know, the teacher *verbalized* or *modeled* one and had the child repeat it.   Yes   No

_____

_____

_____

3. Teacher asked the child to *practice* the appropriate behavior.   Yes   No

_____

_____

4. Teacher gave the child *Positive Feedback* for *any* improvement.   Yes   No

_____

_____

5. Teacher gave the child *homework*.   Yes   No

_____

_____

_____

Most of the time you will use the Teaching Interaction as you have learned it here. It does, however, lend itself nicely to some variations which might be helpful in some situations. For instance, if in the practice section, a child makes some improvement but not as much as you'd like, you can use a Teaching Interaction within a Teaching Interaction as illustrated by the following vignette:

Teacher:
Cory, would you please put up the game now.

Cory:
(whining voice) Oh, all right! (slams the box down)

Teacher:
Cory, thank you for beginning to follow my instructions right away. It would be much better if you used a good attitude. I'll ask you again, and you show me how you can follow directions with a good attitude... Cory, would you please put the game up now.

Cory:
(puts game away, says nothing, does not look at teacher)

Teacher:
Cory, that's much better. You followed my directions without whining. It would have been even better if you would have looked at me and said, "OK" in a nice voice. I want you to practice doing that now. I want you to put the game away now, Cory.

Cory:
OK. (looks at teacher with a pleasant face)

Teacher:
Great! That time you did it perfectly. Next time I give you directions, I want you to do it just like that, remembering to say "OK" and to use a good attitude.

Cory:
OK.

Activity 19. Vignettes for Role Playing the Teaching Interaction

Role play the following vignettes with your partner, alternating the teacher and child parts. Use the Evaluation Checksheet which follows.

You're talking with a child after school. Another child approaches you and interrupts the conversation by asking a question about an assignment, etc.

A child tattles to you about other children calling her names. You want the child to solve her own problem without tattling.

You ask a child to put away his game and the child whines, "Oh, all right."

A child who primarily interacts with adults comes to you and asks you to play at recess. You want the child to play with her peers.

You are checking a child's homework. The answers are correct, but the paper is very messy.

You give directions to a child. The child responds with a good attitude but does not begin the task.

You are talking over an assignment with a child. The child answers and asks questions but does not look at you during the conversation.

Each day one of your children wears clean clothes but forgets to comb her hair and wash her face.

You give directions to a child. The child starts right away with a good attitude, but within a matter of minutes he is out of his seat roaming around the room.

You are talking to a small group of children about a new project. One child volunteers many times, but each time she raises her hand, she says, "Oh, oh, oh!"

You're correcting a child's homework. You ask the child about one answer. He responds by looking at you but answers the question with a bad attitude.

Evaluation Checksheet: The Teaching Interaction

Instructions:

Observe your partner role play. Watch for the correct use of each component. Circle *Yes* if the component was done completely and correctly. Use the lines to write exactly what made it correct. Circle *No* if all or parts of the component were incorrect or incomplete. Describe what could have happened to make it correct.

1. Teacher stopped the interaction by *saying something positive* that was related to the situation.

   Yes   No

   _____

   _____

   _____

2. Teacher asked the child for an *alternative way of behaving*. If the child didn't know, the teacher *verbalized* or *modeled* one and had the child repeat it.

   Yes   No

   _____

   _____

   _____

3. Teacher asked the child to *practice* the appropriate behavior.

   Yes   No

   _____

   _____

   _____

4. Teacher gave the child *Positive Feedback* for *any* improvement.

   Yes   No

   _____

   _____

   _____

5. Teacher gave the child *homework*.

   Yes   No

   _____

   _____

   _____

Activity 20. Homework for the Teaching Interaction

Complete the following Homework exercise in a real setting. Compare your use of the strategy with the components listed in Activity 16.

Within the next day or so, find five situations in which you can use the Teaching Interaction. In the spaces provided, specifically describe each of the situations and exactly what you said in using the Teaching Interaction.

Situation 1: _____

_____

   What I said: _____

_____

Situation 2: _____

_____

   What I said: _____

_____

Situation 3: _____

_____

   What I said: _____

_____

Situation 4: _____

_____

   What I said: _____

_____

Situation 5: _____

_____

   What I said: _____

_____

Direct Prompt

Description

The Direct Prompt is a quick, brief statement that tells the child exactly what he should be doing. You use it when you have tried Ignore-Attend-Praise without success or when a statement whispered into the child's ear without interruption of the flow of the group seems appropriate. After you make the prompt, watch for the appropriate behavior and praise the child.

Use

The Direct Prompt can be a quick and effective way of influencing the child's behavior. In using the Direct Prompt, calmly tell the child exactly what he needs to do in order to be correct. There are several dangers, however, in using the Direct Prompt. If you give it with a slightly negative tone of voice, or if you use it more than once for a given behavior, the Direct Prompt can degenerate to a "nag." Avoid this by keeping a calm voice.

Use the Direct Prompt only if you think a child has not caught on to an Ignore-Attend-Praise sequence, and/or if the Teaching Interaction seems too lengthy for the situation. The main purpose of the Direct Prompt is to inform the child of the behavior expected of him. As with Ignore-Attend-Praise, always follow up by watching for the desired behavior and giving Positive Feedback for its occurrence. You may use the Direct Prompt any time the Ignore-Attend-Praise sequence has not worked and the child's behavior seems to be based on a lack of awareness about what is expected. If the child seems to need to *learn* the skill, you should probably use the Teaching Interaction. If the child seems to be noncompliant about using a skill he *knows*, use the Direct Prompt to make sure the child is informed of the desired behavior. If the child fails to respond to a Direct Prompt, consider him to be noncompliant and then use Sit and Watch (which will be explained shortly).

Activity 21. Memorizing the Components

To use the Direct Prompt:

1. Use a *calm voice* and *eye contact*.

2. Make a *brief statement* about the behavior that is desired (e.g., "You need to keep your hands to yourself").

3. *Watch for the appropriate behavior* and *praise the child*.

Activity 22. Right-Way Vignette for the Direct Prompt

When used correctly, the strategy should look like this:

After the teacher praised the others in the group for keeping their hands still, John continues to play with his shoe-strings.

Teacher:
(with a calm voice and eye contact) John, you need to keep your hands still and fold them in your lap.

(The child complies.)

Teacher:
Good. Now you have nice still hands, John.

Describe how the components of the Direct Prompt were used correctly in this example.

Activity 23. Discrimination Training for the Direct Prompt

Read the following vignettes. Notice if each component is used correctly. Circle *Yes* if the component was done completely and correctly. Use the lines to write exactly what made it correct. Circle *No* if all or parts of the component were incorrect or incomplete. Use the lines to describe what could have happened to make it correct. Check your answers for each vignette against those in Appendix B before going to the next vignette.

The setting for these vignettes is as follows:

Children and teachers are involved in a group lesson; all children are attending and have been praised except John, who is playing with his shoestrings.

Vignette 1

Teacher:
(with eye contact) John, you're not paying attention at all!

1. Teacher used a *calm voice* and *eye contact*. Yes No

_____

_____

_____

2. Teacher made a *brief statement* about the behavior that is desired Yes No
    (e.g., "You need to keep your hands to yourself").

_____

_____

_____

3. Teacher *watched for the appropriate behavior* and *praised the child*. Yes No

_____

_____

_____

Vignette 2

Teacher:
(with a calm voice and eye contact) John, you need to keep your hands in your lap. If you do that, I'll know that you're paying attention to me, and you'll get better scores on your Home Note.

(The child follows directions.)

1. Teacher used a *calm voice* and *eye contact*. Yes No

_____

_____

_____

2. Teacher made a *brief statement* about the behavior that is desired
   (e.g., "You need to keep your hands to yourself").   Yes   No

   _____

   _____

   _____

3. Teacher *watched for the appropriate behavior* and *praised the child*.   Yes   No

   _____

   _____

   _____

Vignette 3:

Teacher:

(with a calm voice and eye contact) John, you need to keep your hands still in your lap.

(The child complies; the teacher continues with the group.)

1. Teacher used a *calm voice* and *eye contact*.   Yes   No

   _____

   _____

   _____

2. Teacher made a *brief statement* about the behavior that is desired
   (e.g., "You need to keep your hands to yourself").   Yes   No

   _____

   _____

   _____

3. Teacher *watched for the appropriate behavior* and *praised the child*.   Yes   No

   _____

   _____

   _____

Activity 24. Vignettes for Role Playing the Direct Prompt

Role play the following vignettes with your partner, alternating the teacher and child parts. Use the Evaluation Checksheet which follows.

A child is not looking at you while you are talking.

In the group, a child is shifting around instead of sitting still.

One child is touching others and has a problem keeping his hands to himself.

A child is playing with clothing (e.g., continuously pulling up socks) instead of paying attention.

A youngster continues to play with a game after directions have been given to clean up.

A child cuts up in line after directions are given to line up at the door.

A child does not stay seated on the bus during a class field trip.

One youngster unties the ribbons from a classmate's hair.

A child takes a classmate's pencil because the child's own pencil was lost.

One child in the group is talking loudly during a classroom film.

A youngster knocks several coats off the rack and does not pick them up.

One child continuously interrupts you as you are trying to help another student read.

One youngster grabs a cookie from another after it has been politely offered.

A child continues to complain after you've used Ignore-Attend-Praise.

Evaluation Checksheet: The Direct Prompt

Instructions:

Observe your partner role play. Watch for correct use of each component. Circle *Yes* if the component was done completely and correctly. Use the lines to write exactly what made it correct. Circle *No* if all or parts of the component were incorrect or incomplete. Describe what could have happened to make it correct.

1. Teacher used a *calm voice* and *eye contact*.   Yes   No

_____

_____

_____

2. Teacher made a *brief statement* about the behavior that is desired   Yes   No
   (e.g., "You need to keep your hands to yourself").

_____

_____

_____

3. Teacher *watched for the appropriate behavior* and *praised the child*.   Yes   No

_____

_____

_____

Activity 25. Homework for the Direct Prompt

Complete the following Homework exercise in a real setting. Compare your use of the strategy with the components listed in Activity 21.

Within the next day or so, find five situations in which you can use the Direct Prompt. In the spaces provided, specifically describe each situation and exactly what you said in using the Direct Prompt.

Situation 1: _____

_____

    What I said: _____

_____

Situation 2: _____

_____

    What I said: _____

_____

Situation 3: _____

_____

    What I said: _____

_____

Situation 4: _____

_____

    What I said: _____

_____

Situation 5: _____

_____

    What I said: _____

_____

Sit and Watch

Description

Sit and Watch is a technique for removing a child from participation when that child has in some way disrupted the group. The Sit and Watch procedure begins with calmly removing the child to a chair on the periphery of the room. The child must then *sit* quietly, maintain a good attitude, and *watch* how the other children in the group engage in appropriate behavior. (Dealing with noncompliance during the Sit and Watch procedure is discussed later.) After the child has watched for 2 minutes, you lead him through an interaction that requires him to name the inappropriate behavior and the desired behavior. You support each of the child's efforts in this process with Positive Feedback. Once you are satisfied that the child is ready to return to the group, you escort the child back and praise appropriate responding.

The chair used for Sit and Watch should be located to serve two purposes: (1) at least one teacher should be able to observe the child at all times and (2) the child should be close enough to the rest of the children to observe them and hear Positive Feedback that is given.

It is very important that Sit and Watch does not become an escape from something that the child finds unpleasant during the group; he should return to the same activity or set of demands that was initially difficult for him.

Use

Sit and Watch is a procedure designed to interrupt disruptive behavior by removal of the child, while providing a learning experience. It is not intended as punishment, though some loss of privileges (such as not earning all of snack time) may result. The time spent away from the group is instructional in that the child is told to watch how his peers appropriately exhibit the behavior he did not. The process for the child returning to the group is also instructional; the child must name the misbehavior and, more importantly, state the desirable behavior. Before the child may return to the group, he must show some appropriate social skills, e.g., use a pleasant face and voice. Once the child returns to the group, he is given the opportunity to use the skill correctly and receive Positive Feedback. Like all other Teaching Strategies, Sit and Watch provides an opportunity for the occurrence of the appropriate skill and Positive Feedback by the teacher.

Sit and Watch is the most restrictive of the Teaching Strategies. Use it only for highly disruptive behaviors (those which attract the attention of both you and peers) when other strategies have been tried unsuccessfully, or for blatant rule violations or noncompliance with your instructions. Do not use Sit and Watch in any setting unless you have first introduced and role played it for the children in a nonthreatening way. Use Sit and Watch very infrequently. During the first few sessions of small-group meetings it may be necessary once or twice, particularly with disruptive or younger children.

Activity 26. Memorizing the Components

To use Sit and Watch:

1. *Remove the child* to the Sit and Watch chair, calmly saying, "_____, you need to sit and watch how the other children (*the desired behavior*, e.g., work quietly without making noises)."

2. *Time the child's wait* in the chair for *2 minutes*.

3. *Praise* others for appropriate behavior.

4. After 2 minutes, *go to the child* and *give Positive Feedback*. Calmly say, "_____, you've been sitting quietly with your hands still."

5. Have the *child name the inappropriate behavior*. Say, "You need to tell me why you're in Sit and Watch." (If the child cannot verbalize the misbehavior, you state it and have the child repeat it.) *Then say*, "Right."

6. Have the *child name the appropriate behavior*. Ask, "What do you need to do when you get back to the group?" (If the child does not name the correct behavior, you state it and have the child repeat it.) *Then say*, "Good for you! You can come back to the group."

7. Once the child is back in the group, *watch for the correct behavior* and *give the child Positive Feedback*.

Activity 27. Right-Way Vignette for Sit and Watch

When used correctly, the strategy should look like this:

It is lesson time, and Billy just pushed the child sitting next to him. The teacher goes over to Billy, escorts him to the Sit and Watch chair, and whispers to him.

Teacher:
Billy, you need to sit and watch how the other children keep their hands to themselves.

(The teacher notes the time and returns to the group.)

Teacher:
John, Sue, and Shawn really look like they're ready to role play; they've been looking right at me and keeping their hands to themselves.

(The 2-minute time period is completed; the teacher approaches the child.)

Teacher:
Billy, you've been sitting quietly. You need to tell me why you're in Sit and Watch.

Billy:
Because I pushed Shawn.

Teacher:
Right. What do you need to do when you get back to the group?

Billy:
Keep my hands to myself.

Teacher:
Good for you. Now you can come back to the group.

Describe how the components of Sit and Watch were correctly used in this example.

Activity 28. Discrimination Training for Sit and Watch

Read the following vignettes. Notice if each component is used correctly. Circle *Yes* if the component was done completely and correctly. Use the lines to write exactly what made it correct. Circle *No* if all or parts of the component were incorrect or incomplete. Use the lines to describe what could have happened to make it correct. Check your answers for each vignette against those in Appendix B before going to the next vignette.

The setting for these vignettes is as follows:
A lesson is in progress. Jim is acting silly, continues to laugh, and tries to get others involved in his silliness.

Vignette 1

Teacher:
Jim, you need to sit and watch because you're really bugging everybody.

(The teacher notes the time and returns to the group. After 2 minutes the teacher returns to Jim and speaks to him.)

Teacher:
Jim, right now you're sitting still. You need to tell me why you're in Sit and Watch.

Child:
Because I was laughing during the session.

Teacher:
Good, Jim, now you're ready to come back to the group.

1. Teacher *removed the child* to the Sit and Watch chair, calmly saying, "_____, you need to sit and watch how the other children (*the desired behavior*, e.g., work quietly without making noise)."   Yes   No

_____

_____

_____

2. Teacher *timed the child's wait* for 2 minutes.   Yes   No

_____

_____

_____

3. Teacher *praised others* for appropriate behavior.   Yes   No

_____

_____

_____

4. After 2 minutes, the teacher *went to the child* and *gave Positive Feedback*, calmly saying, "_____, you've been sitting quietly with your hands still."   Yes   No

_____

_____

_____

5. Teacher *had the child name the inappropriate behavior*, saying,
   "You need to tell me why you're in Sit and Watch." (If the child
   couldn't name the misbehavior, the teacher stated it and had the
   child repeat it.) Then the teacher *said*, "Right."   Yes   No

   _____

   _____

   _____

6. Teacher *had the child name the appropriate behavior*, saying,
   "What do you need to do when you get back to the group?" (If
   the child couldn't name the correct behavior, the teacher stated
   it and had the child repeat it.) Then the teacher *said*, "Good for
   you. You can come back to the group now."   Yes   No

   _____

   _____

   _____

7. After the child returned to the group, the teacher *watched for the
   correct behavior* and *gave Positive Feedback for the child's
   correct behavior*.   Yes   No

   _____

   _____

   _____

Vignette 2

Teacher:
Jim, you need to sit and watch how the others are paying attention to the lesson and being serious.

(The teacher notes the time and returns to the group. After 2 minutes the teacher returns to Jim and speaks to him.)

Teacher:
Jim, you need to tell me why you're in Sit and Watch.

Child:
Because I was laughing during the lesson.

Teacher:
What do you need to do when you get back to the group?

Child:
Pay attention to the teacher and stop laughing.

Teacher:
Good, Jim, now you're ready to come back to the group.

1. Teacher *removed the child* to the Sit and Watch chair, calmly saying,
   "_____, you need to sit and watch how the other
   children (*the desired behavior*, e.g., work quietly without making
   noise)."   Yes   No

   _____

   _____

   _____

2. Teacher *timed the child's wait* for *2* minutes.   Yes   No

_____

_____

_____

3. Teacher *praised others* for appropriate behavior.   Yes   No

_____

_____

_____

4. After 2 minutes, the teacher *went to the child* and *gave Positive Feed-back,* calmly saying, "_____, you've been sitting quietly with your hands still."   Yes   No

_____

_____

_____

5. Teacher *had the child name the inappropriate behavior*, saying, "You need to tell me why you're in Sit and Watch." (If the child couldn't name the misbehavior, the teacher stated it and had the child repeat it.) Then the teacher *said*, "Right."   Yes   No

_____

_____

_____

6. Teacher *had the child name the appropriate behavior*, saying, "What do you need to do when you get back to the group?" (If the child couldn't name the correct behavior, the teacher stated it and had the child repeat it.) Then the teacher *said*, "Good for you. You can come back to the group now."   Yes   No

_____

_____

_____

7. After the child returned to the group, the teacher *watched for the correct behavior* and *gave Positive Feedback for the child's correct behavior*.   Yes   No

_____

_____

_____

Vignette 3

Teacher:
You need to sit and watch.

(The teacher notes the time and returns to the group. After 2 minutes the teacher returns to Jim and speaks to him.)

Teacher:
Jim, you need to tell me why you're in Sit and Watch.

Child:
Because I was laughing.

Teacher:
What do you need to do to get back to the group?

Child:
Pay attention.

Teacher:
OK, come back to the group.

1. Teacher *removed the child* to the Sit and Watch chair, calmly saying, "_____, you need to sit and watch how the other children (*the desired behavior*, e.g., work quietly without making noise)."   Yes   No

_____

_____

_____

2. Teacher *timed the child's wait* for *2* minutes.   Yes   No

_____

_____

_____

3. Teacher *praised others* for appropriate behavior.   Yes   No

_____

_____

_____

4. After 2 minutes, the teacher *went to the child* and *gave Positive Feedback*, calmly saying, "_____, you've been sitting quietly with your hands still."   Yes   No

_____

_____

_____

5. Teacher *had the child name the inappropriate behavior*, saying, "You need to tell me why you're in Sit and Watch." (If the child couldn't name the misbehavior, the teacher stated it and had the child repeat it.) Then the teacher *said*, "Right."   Yes   No

_____

_____

_____

6. Teacher *had the child name the appropriate behavior*, saying, "What do you need to do when you get back to the group?" (If the child couldn't name the correct behavior, the teacher stated it and had the child repeat it.) Then the teacher *said*, "Good for you. You can come back to the group now."

Yes   No

_____

_____

_____

7. After the child returned to the group, the teacher *watched for the correct behavior* and *gave Positive Feedback for the child's correct behavior*.

Yes   No

_____

_____

_____

_____

Repeated use of Sit and Watch (several times in a group period or over several sessions) may indicate other problems. Examine the environment; in order for removal from participation to be a powerful consequence, the group must be a desirable place to be. If this seems to be true for most children in your setting, carefully observe the child or children with whom you are using Sit and Watch. Some children are more powerfully motivated by other factors. For example, a severely withdrawn child might find Sit and Watch to be a reprieve from the role play and group performance. Another child might find the fun of giggling and distracting other children more exciting than participating in group and snack time. Keep your use of Sit and Watch in perspective with your overall goals for the children. Remember, the focus at all times is to facilitate success for children and promote acquisition of new skills. Sit and Watch, like the other Teaching Strategies, should be used only as it meets this goal. In your efforts to problem solve difficult situations, outside observers can be extremely helpful; don't hesitate to use these resources, especially if you know someone who has also been trained in this program.

There may be occasions when the child is so emotionally involved that he will not calm down within the 2-minute Sit and Watch period. Use the following guidelines in dealing with these problems.

If the child is not calm, has not been sitting quietly, or does not answer you with a good attitude, calmly say, "_____, you need to sit here quietly for another 2 minutes. When I come back, you need to be calm and show a good attitude." Return to the group, and attend to appropriate behavior for 2 minutes. If the child has not been calm or shown a good attitude, repeat the previous step. If he is quiet, return to the child and say, "You've been sitting quietly, _____. You need to tell me why you are in Sit and Watch." If the child answers to your satisfaction, continue taking him out of Sit and Watch according to the procedure. If he does not, repeat this process. In rare instances, with a child who is extremely upset or violent, the process may take 20 minutes or longer. While the child is in Sit and Watch, he is not engaging in behaviors that earn privileges such as snack time. You may wish to remind the other children of how they *are* earning privileges. If the child continues not to respond, you will want to examine the individual case more carefully.

Activity 29. Vignettes for Role Playing Sit and Watch

Role play the following vignettes with your partner, alternating the teacher and child parts. Use the Evaluation Checksheet which follows.

One child pushes another child down on the playground.

A youngster continuously talks out after being prompted to keep a quiet mouth.

A group of children are playing a board game; one child gets mad and throws a piece of the game at another child.

One child trips another as he walks by.

During the lesson one child continuously makes faces at the other children to get their attention.

One child continues to look around after being prompted to pay attention by looking at the speaker.

You give some directions to a child; the child argues and has a bad attitude. You respond by using the Teaching Interaction, but the child continues to argue and then starts stomping his feet.

When you give instructions for the children to put away an art activity, all of them comply except one, who says, "No!" in an angry voice.

You have just gone over the playground rules with your class. When you go outside, you see one person throwing sand at other children.

During art time you see a child snip off some of his classmate's hair with his scissors.

At the lunch table you see a child smash another's dessert with his fork.

One person has just fallen down in the mud. When he gets up, he wipes his hands on a child standing nearby.

During a game, a child screams in his partner's ear.

Evaluation Checksheet: Sit and Watch

Instructions:

Observe your partner role play. Watch for the correct use of each component. Circle *Yes* if the component was done completely and correctly. Use the lines to write exactly what made it correct. Circle *No* if all or parts of the component were incorrect or incomplete. Describe what could have happened to make it correct.

1. Teacher *removed the child* to the Sit and Watch chair, calmly saying,   Yes   No
   "_____, you need to sit and watch how the other
   children (*the desired behavior*, e.g., work quietly without making
   noise)."

   _____

   _____

   _____

2. Teacher *timed the child's wait* for *2* minutes.   Yes   No

   _____

   _____

   _____

3. Teacher *praised others* for appropriate behavior.   Yes   No

   _____

   _____

   _____

4. After 2 minutes, the teacher *went to the child* and *gave Positive Feed-*   Yes   No
   back, calmly saying, "_____, you've been sitting quietly
   with your hands still."

   _____

   _____

   _____

5. Teacher *had the child name the inappropriate behavior*, saying,   Yes   No
   "You need to tell me why you're in Sit and Watch." (If the child
   couldn't name the misbehavior, the teacher stated it and had the
   child repeat it.) Then the teacher *said*, "Right."

   _____

   _____

   _____

6. Teacher *had the child name the appropriate behavior*, saying, "What do you need to do when you get back to the group?" (If the child couldn't name the correct behavior, the teacher stated it and had the child repeat it.) Then the teacher *said*, "Good for you. You can come back to the group now."

Yes   No

_____

_____

_____

7. After the child returned to the group, the teacher *watched for the correct behavior* and *gave Positive Feedback for the child's correct behavior*.

Yes   No

_____

_____

_____

Activity 30. Homework for Sit and Watch

Because Sit and Watch should be used only as a last resort, it would be inappropriate to encourage its use in real settings for the sake of practice. Instead, complete the following questions and compare your answers to those in Appendix B.

1. You have just used Sit and Watch with a child in your group who refused to role play. What should you do when you bring him back to the group?

_____

_____

_____

2. A child in your group just pinched another child. This is the first time this child has done anything of this sort. What Teaching Strategy would you use? Give your rationale.

_____

_____

_____

3. What would you change about this physical arrangement?

_____

_____

_____

Sit and Watch
chair

teacher

Guidelines for Using the Teaching Strategies

The five Teaching Strategies are organized in a hierarchy ranging from skills that require the child to take the major responsibility for her behavior to techniques that are more teacher directed. As you are using the program, you will constantly be faced with deciding which strategy will maximize the teaching opportunity at hand. This becomes second nature after practice. However, the protocol that follows may be helpful in getting you started. Think of the skills along a continuum as in the following illustration. Consider the parallel continuum of child responsibility. In each situation with a child, your decision about how to handle it should be based on an understanding of the child's abilities; always choose the strategy that invests the greatest amount of responsibility in the child without threatening opportunities for success. For example, if you judged that Sarah knew she should raise her hand quietly before speaking, you would use Ignore-Attend-Praise to build that behavior. If you tried Ignore-Attend-Praise and she did not respond, you would try the Direct Prompt. On the other hand, if you didn't think she was aware that she should raise her hand and be called on before speaking, you would probably use the Teaching Interaction.

Keep these levels of child vs. teacher-directed behavior in mind and follow the specific suggestions for "use" provided for each Teaching Strategy.

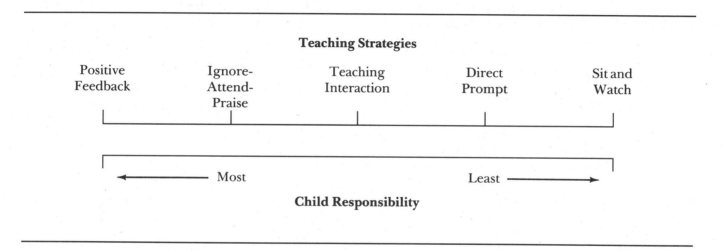

Additional Teaching Techniques

In addition to learning to use the five Teaching Strategies, you should learn to use the following additional techniques. These provide protocols for dealing with specific problematic situations including: (1) getting the children "ready," (2) making transitions run smoothly, (3) rehearsing for high-risk settings, (4) making privileges contingent, (5) teaching children to "take responsibility,"* (6) teaching problem solving,* (7) using a verbal prompting sequence, (8) using physical prompting, and (9) using coaching.

Getting the Children "Ready"

Fun activities may increase the risk of your losing instructional control. It is important that children loosen up enough to show their true colors, thereby giving you opportunities to help them improve their social skills. Yet if there are too many behaviors occurring, you will not be able to attend to them all. Inappropriate behaviors will occur without the advantage of being corrected and replaced with positive behaviors. In these situations the technique of getting the children "ready" can help you maintain a workable level of behavior.

Getting ready is used especially when children are engaged in, or are about to engage in, a preferred activity. The children understand that the privilege of doing something they prefer is contingent on first exhibiting, and then maintaining, a certain level of appropriate (or ready) behaviors. Although ready behaviors may vary according to the activity, they typically would include:

1. Good attitude.
2. Listening skills.
3. Following directions.
4. Cooperation.

If you are explaining the rules of a new game to the children, they need to show that they are ready to hear the rules by exhibiting good listening behaviors. If you notice that only two of six children are listening, you may use a sequence like this:

Teacher:
Jack and Jill, you are showing me that you are ready to learn about the game because you are looking at me and not interrupting. When we go outside, you can be first to choose teams.

(Other children then show ready behaviors.)

Teacher:
Good, now everyone is quiet and looking at me. Now I will be able to explain the game.

You will notice that because in this example some children were exhibiting the ready behaviors, the teacher used the Ignore-Attend-Praise sequence by *ignoring* the children who were not ready, *attending* to the children who were, and then *praising* the children who got ready. Also, her attending to the ready children was in the form of Positive Feedback. In this way, all of the children got to hear what behaviors were expected.

If no children are exhibiting the ready behaviors, you might use a Direct Prompt to the group. It could sound something like this:

Teacher:
Everyone needs to show me he or she is ready to hear about our new game by looking at me and keeping quiet mouths.

(The children show ready behaviors.)

Teacher:
Good, now everyone is quiet and looking at me. Now I know you are all listening.

In the preceding example, the teacher identified the behaviors she considered to show readiness. Instead she might use the same Direct Prompt, but not name the ready behaviors. That might sound something like this:

Teacher:
Everyone needs to show me he or she is ready to hear about our new game. How could you do that?

(The children show ready behaviors.)

Teacher:
Good, now everyone is quiet and looking at me. Now I know you are all listening.

If the children are *already engaged* in a preferred activity and any of them begin to have problems cooperating, following directions, etc., you may prompt for the ready behaviors in order that they may continue to participate in the preferred activity. There will be times in this type of situation, however, when the level of inappropriate behavior cannot be successfully dealt with by mere prompting or the use of Ignore-Attend-Praise. If you've already tried these two strategies unsuccessfully, or if you judge the situation warrants a stronger intervention, you may need to intervene and use the Teaching Interaction to teach the more appropriate behavior. To do so, you will need

---

*These additional techniques are named for the specific behavior problems they address. These titles also refer to target behaviors and core skills.

60

the children's complete attention. However, when a negative interaction is occurring in relation to a preferred activity, it is very difficult for you to draw the children's attention away from the activity and to yourself. In order to do this in a neutral way, you can, without saying anything to the children, simply remove the activity or an essential component of the activity, thus allowing the children to focus complete attention on you. In the case of a board game, you can pick up the spinner or dice or close the board. In the case of snacks, you can remove the food or push it away from the children to the center of the table. For arts or crafts activities, you can remove the essential tools or materials. After the children have responded appropriately to the Teaching Interaction and are exhibiting the ready behaviors, you replace those items that you had removed and the activity resumes. If there is a subsequent problem with the activity, discontinue it and try it again on another occasion. Always take care to use a pleasant voice and Positive Feedback.

Making Transitions Run Smoothly

The transition from one activity to another is typically a time for children in groups to have problems following directions, listening, cooperating, etc. In order to ensure that these transition times go more smoothly, you can do several things. Choose those children who are ready to have the special privileges in the next activity. When doing this, be careful to give Positive Feedback so that the ready children are reinforced for specific behaviors while the children who were not ready get to hear what behaviors are expected. You can also dismiss the children one at a time to go to the next activity, giving each one a specific task in order to prepare for that activity. In this way, the children's energy is focused, and the transition is smooth. It is always a good idea when two teachers are working together for one teacher to go to the next activity to "receive" the children as they arrive.

Rehearsing for High-Risk Settings

Just prior to a social situation in which a child typically has a problem, you and the child can engage in rehearsal. If, for example, a particular child is teased on the playground and has a difficult time ignoring it and staying calm, you will take the child aside before recess, describe a teasing vignette, and then ask the child to *verbalize* what to say or do. After verbalization about what to say or do, you role play it with the child and then praise the child for staying calm and practicing. Then tell the child that you will be watching to see how it goes on the playground. (If this is not possible, tell the child that right after recess you are going to ask

how it went.) After recess, praise any attempts at the new behaviors.

This entire sequence can be outlined as follows:

1. Teacher describes a problem situation and asks child what to do or say.
2. Child verbalizes possible coping behaviors (with teacher's help if necessary).
3. Child practices with teacher.
4. Teacher praises child's practice efforts.
5. Teacher gives child "homework" (i.e., "Now go out and try it").
6. Teacher observes and reinforces.

Making Privileges Contingent

During development of the program we have frequently used the statement "Nothing's free" to describe our contingent use of virtually anything in the environment that could be viewed as a privilege. From choosing children to answer questions to assigning special helpers at snack time, any and all opportunities for special attention are awarded contingently upon appropriate or improved behavior. Using both small as well as more meaningful daily activities to underline progress made by children adds an extremely important measure of effectiveness to implementing the program. The child who remains calm during relaxation training would be chosen to turn on the lights. The children sending the best "I'm interested" messages would be selected to role play first. The child standing the most quietly in line would get to take the basketball out to the playground. There are literally hundreds of opportunities such as these for you to take advantage of. Of course, each privilege is given along with Positive Feedback which specifies how the child earned the privilege: "Jason, since you followed all the directions during relaxation, you may go and turn on the light."

Along the same line, contingent use of snack time can play an important part in motivating the children. Since having and serving snacks is almost always of great interest to the children, snack time provides many opportunities for you to manipulate contingencies. A very effective way of motivating the children is to make snack time contingent upon the child's reaching competence (to your satisfaction) in following the classroom rules and role playing the day's skills. Those children who reach competency during skill lesson time may then go to snack and may be given special jobs for setting up the snack. Children who have not yet reached competency when snack time arrives will use some or all of the time practicing in their particular area of weakness until they display the lacking skill. When you feel the child has mastered the skill, you can excuse her to snack time. A natural set of consequences comes into play here; those arriving late have less time, and there is less of the snack available to them.

Teaching Children to "Take Responsibility"

In teaching social skills, we have found blaming and excuse making to be major problems – some that are frequently modeled by parents and teachers. Therefore, it is very important to recognize and praise those children who take responsibility for their behavior. For example, even though a child may have been *irresponsible* and forgotten the day's Homework, you praise the child for taking verbal responsibility if he simply says, "I forgot it," when asked about it. You praise the child for telling the truth and not making excuses. You then help the child problem solve to think of a way to remember Homework in the future. Accepting the prearranged consequences is another important component of taking responsibility. The child who forgets Homework, does not make excuses, and has a good attitude about finishing Homework while the others have free play is being responsible. Try to make the prearranged consequence related to the typical problems that occur. When both you and the children expect these contingencies to be applied in a matter-of-fact way, unpleasant episodes of arguing and excuse making are avoided (see target behavior I take responsibility for myself, Chapter 3).

Teaching Problem Solving

Many children typically react to their problems in ineffective ways. Some might cry; others might hit; still others might tattle to adults. These responses do little to help children find satisfying solutions to their problems. In fact, they often create new problems. You can help children solve problems by using the interaction sequence that follows. The sequence encourages the child to solve her own problem in a responsible manner by (1) getting calm; (2) thinking of at least three ideas; (3) choosing the best one for her by thinking about what might happen; and (4) trying that one first.

Child:
Cindy is teasing me and calling me names!

Adult:
That sounds like a problem. What's the first thing you can do to begin solving the problem?

Child:
I could take a deep breath to get my body calm.

Adult:
Right, you can first get calm. Then what are at least three different things you can do to make the problem better for you?

Child:
I can ignore her and find someone else to play with.

Adult:
Those are two really good ideas.

Child:
But I really feel like hitting her!

Adult:
Will that make the problem better or worse for you?

Child:
The problem would get worse because we would get into a fight.

Adult:
Right. Another thing you could do is tell on her, but what happens when you tell on other children a lot?

Child:
You lose friends because they think you are a tattletale.

Adult:
I think you're right. So what is the best solution for you?

Child:
Ignore her and find someone else to play with.

Adult:
That solution sounds like it might really solve your problem. Thanks for practicing that with me with such a good attitude. I'd like you to try that right now, and later I will ask you how it went.

Using a Verbal Prompting Sequence

Often a child's ability to answer a question is improved with gentle assistance from you. Such prompting can assure that each interaction ends with successful execution of the desired response. An equally important goal, however, is to have the children become independent thinkers so that they can problem solve on their own. The prompting sequence achieves these goals through three levels of assistance, ranging from virtually no prompts to very structured prompts. The sequence is especially useful when asking children to describe components of the behaviors exhibited in role plays.

Level One – Open-Ended Questions. All questioning begins with Level One, an open-ended question which provides the children with opportunities to supply the largest amount of information on their own with the least amount of prompting. At the end of each of the role plays the lead teacher asks an open-ended question. For example, you ask, "How did you know that was the right way to do that?" or "Who has some feedback for _____?" or "What did _____ do that was the right way to interrupt?"

A child's answers should describe the day's objectives (or their absence in "wrong-way" examples). If children do not describe the behaviors exactly at this point, go on to Level Two.

Level Two – Leading Questions. In the second level of the prompting sequence, a bit more structure is provided, giving the children less responsibility for describing behaviors on their own. For example, if the component was "looking at the other person," you would prompt by asking, "Where was _____ looking?" If the component to be described was "waiting for a pause in the conversation," you might ask, "What did _____ do while they were talking?"

Level Three – Yes/No Questions. In Level Three, the children's responses are structured still further. You ask a question that requires a yes/no answer: "Did _____ look at _____?" or "Did _____ wait for a pause?" After a child answers correctly, you have the child repeat the entire statement, e.g., "He was looking at her with a pleasant face" or "Shawn, you did a good job because you waited for a pause."

It is important to note that verbalizing *about* the skill should be minimized. Persistence in this area should be avoided, especially if it threatens to use time allocated for actual practice. If, in your judgment, children are unlikely to be able to articulate answers (especially if they are very young), you may expedite the process by going directly to Level Three or even telling the children the answer and having them repeat it.

Using Physical Prompting

In order to practice and learn new behaviors, some children need modeling and physical prompting from the teacher. For example, if a child is learning to raise his hand to volunteer, but does not do this with verbal prompting, you can ask a question, raise your own hand to *model* the expected behavior, and *hold up* the child's hand with yours. You then praise the child for volunteering. If the behavior to be learned is eye contact with the speaker, you gently lift the child's chin and point in the direction of the speaker. Physical prompting can be used for many other behaviors that a child is slow to learn.

When working in a small group, you can make the physical prompting more efficient by placing those children who need it most on either side of you. In this way prompting is done without disturbing the other group members.

When working with a large group, walk among the students, making sure you are near the student(s) needing the prompting at the appropriate time.

Physical prompts are always done gently and should be followed with some supportive physical contact, such as a pat on the back, and Positive Feedback.

Using Coaching

There will be times when you will want a child to practice a more appropriate social behavior during the Teaching Interaction, role play setting, in response to a peer, etc., and he will have difficulty doing it due to immaturity, shyness, confusion, lack of motivation, or other factors. For example, the following might happen in a role play situation:

(You have just given Jerome instructions to role play; he is to pretend Teacher 2 is his mother. She had just offered to help him fix his bike.)

Teacher 2:
Jerome, I'm sorry to see your tire is flat. Would you like a ride to the service station to get some air in it?

Jerome:
(stares blankly at Teacher 2)

In a situation like this you will need to coach the child to ensure successful practice efforts. This can be done by standing very near or behind him, placing a hand on his shoulder or back, and using one of the two techniques illustrated by the following examples, i.e., (1) whispering instructions or (2) feeding actual verbatim responses for him to repeat.

Example (1)

(Teacher 1 moves behind Jerome and whispers, "Tell your mom 'Thank you,' and what you liked.")

Example (2)

(Teacher 1 moves behind Jerome and whispers, "Say, 'Thanks, Mom, for helping me out.'")

If the child is not looking at the person he is interacting with, you can use physical prompting by gently lifting or turning his chin so that he is directly facing the other person. After he has completed the interaction once with coaching, provide Positive Feedback and have him repeat the interaction with little or no coaching. Then be sure to provide Positive Feedback for specific elements of the interaction, willingness to practice, calm body, and good attitude. Remember coaching is intended to encourage a successful, supportive learning experience. Therefore, children are only required to practice as much as their individual capabilities dictate. Keep in mind individual maturation and frustrational levels.

Program Guidelines

The overriding purpose of this program has been to create a positive, supportive, and *fair* environment in which children will feel secure, have some fun, and be motivated to learn. During the program's developmental years, we tried many different strategies for achieving this goal. As we gained more and more experience, it became clear that the approaches shown in the following guidelines were consistently effective in creating such an environment. We therefore encourage your use of these guidelines in addition to the techniques previously described.

Program Guidelines: Rules We Live By

1. Always get positive closure in every interaction with the children.

2. Make *all* interactions between teachers in the presence of the children a model of the program.

3. Avoid arguing, raising your voice or showing sarcasm with the children (always model a good attitude).

4. Use Sit and Watch without show of emotion.

5. Apply rules consistently.

6. Make special privileges (helping teacher, etc.) contingent. Always tell children why they are being chosen for special privileges.

7. Always deliver reinforcers you have promised.

8. Require children to exhibit good attitudes and good listening skills when interacting with you or other children in the group.

9. Never leave children unsupervised.

10. Require that children show that they are *ready* in order to engage in a particular activity.

11. You and the other teacher always support each other.

12. Do not reinforce off-task or inappropriate verbal behavior, such as blaming, making excuses, gossiping, etc., by attending to it. Use a Teaching Strategy to require practice of more appropriate verbal behavior.

13. Require children who have not been listening, who don't know the answers to a question, or who don't know what directions were given to take responsibility for that and say, "I don't know" or, "I wasn't listening," etc.

14. When the group begins, limit your focus to the group only and take advantage of every opportunity to work with the children.

Chapter 5

Introducing and Practicing New Skills

The program is designed to take best advantage of existing opportunities for teaching social skills, as well as structure the initial acquisition of new skills. The Teaching Strategies (Chapter 4) are for capturing natural learning opportunities and strengthening social skills in any setting. The present chapter details the structured skill lesson which provides for the initial presentation of each new skill. Other activities are also described which help you create settings for practicing new skills.

Skill Lesson

Overviewing the Skill Lesson

The skill lesson is a plan for introducing new skills; virtually any well-defined skill may be presented in this manner. The 17 identified social skills of the program have been written into skill lessons. The skill lessons have a very structured format which allows clear introduction and demonstration of new skills, as well as structured practice. Introducing new skills according to this format has numerous advantages. It allows the child to master new skills in a supportive situation. Thus, the child can thoroughly learn the components of a new approach before attempting it while emotionally involved.

The major focus is on child behavior. Thirty minutes of the session is devoted to structured learning of a new skill. You should ensure that most of that time (20 minutes) is reserved for the children to practice the new skill in role play situations. The Teaching Strategies are used during the skill lesson for improving children's spontaneous social behavior, as well as for group behavior management. The vocabulary used in the skill lesson is designed to cut across age groups and functioning levels and to focus on the positive. The skill lesson also deals with conceptual issues:

labels are provided with clear referents; rationales are discussed so that children can see how using the skill may benefit them; and a dose of the real world is given through the reality check to help counteract the non-supportive environment children might face.

Learning to Use the Skill Lesson

On the following pages are two learning devices – (1) Components of the Skill Lesson: Overview, and (2) Skill Lesson Format. They are designed to help you become thoroughly familiar with the basic components of the skill lesson. The overview describes the components and offers cautions and rationales for each. The overview is keyed to the skill lessons by the boldfaced, bulleted section headings (refer to example session outline at the end of this chapter). Once you have familiarized yourself with the concepts described in the overview, move on to the Skill Lesson Format. The Skill Lesson Format provides the lead-in statements you will use in each of the skill lessons. It is also keyed to the skill lesson by the boldfaced, bulleted section headings.

To facilitate your learning, we have broken the skill lesson into five parts, including: (1) introduction – the skill is labeled and defined, (2) demonstration – instances and noninstances of the skill are demonstrated and discussed, (3) practice – the children practice the skill in individualized role play situations, (4) rationales – benefits of using the skill are discussed, and (5) reality check – potential problems are discussed. The part designations appear only in the Overview and the Skill Lesson Format to aid your learning; they are not shown in the skill lessons themselves. Once you memorize the italicized parts of the Skill Lesson Format, you will find that preparing to teach each day's skill is a simple matter of inserting the new material pertinent to that skill according to the script provided in the skill lessons themselves.

Components of the Skill Lesson: Overview

Part One – Introduction

● **Introduce skill and list components.**

You as teacher label the day's topic and list the components of the day's skill. Keep this short and simple. Additional talking *about* the skill wastes valuable role play time.

Part Two – Demonstration

● **Role play appropriate example.**

You and your fellow teacher role play the right way to do the day's skill.

● **Ask children for behavior components of skill.**

Children practice naming components of the skill by giving Positive Feedback. If the child focuses on the negative, i.e., says, "You didn't argue," or "You didn't have a whiny voice," instead of "You had a good attitude," prompt for a more positive answer. Do this by using a Teaching Interaction to have the child practice saying the positive statement. Like other instances where behavior is talked about, this should be limited. Prompting for correct answers should follow the verbal prompting sequence noted in Chapter 4.

● **Role play inappropriate example.**

Again, you and your fellow teacher role play the day's skill, but this time you show the wrong way to do it. You are actually highlighting the differences between instances and noninstances of the skill.

● **Ask children for behavior components of skill.**

You will need to keep this part brief, prompting them as necessary. Their participation at this point is important in carrying through the discrimination training and in helping to emphasize the components of the behavior.

Note that role plays are carefully designed to be limited to the behavior to be learned and to not confuse the children with other issues. The prompts provided in the script encourage children to look for the positive as they name the components.

Part Three – Practice

● **Ask children to role play.**

Give the children vignette situations to role play. This is the most important part of the skill lesson; as many children as possible should role play at least one example. Children give each other Positive Feedback about the use of behavior components in the role play. They give Positive Feedback directly to the person (e.g., the child looks at the person and says, "You remembered to wait for a pause. . ." rather than looking at you and saying, "He. . . ").

Part Four – Rationales

● **Ask children for rationales for using skill.**

Here you prompt children to describe rationales for using the skill. It is important that children see the relationship between their use of new skills and possible positive consequences.

Part Five – Reality Check

● **Lead children through reality check.**

You and your fellow teacher role play a possible real situation in which the use of a new skill does not result in the desired response from the other person. The children generate ideas of what to do if this happens. Prompt as necessary. Remind children that keeping calm in a situation like this can help them solve problems more easily.

Skill Lesson Format

Part One – Introduction
● **Introduce skill and list components.**
"Today we are going to talk about _____."

Part Two – Demonstration
● **Role play appropriate example.**
"This is the right way to _____."
● **Ask children for behavior components of skill.**
"How did you know that was the right way to _____?"
● **Role play inappropriate example.**
"This is the wrong way to _____."
● **Ask children for behavior components of skill.**
"What should have happened to make that the right way to _____?"

Part Three – Practice
● **Ask children to role play.**

"Now it is your turn to role play." (Assign role play situation.)
● **Ask children to give Positive Feedback.**
"Good role playing. Who can give _____ some Positive Feedback on his/her role play?"
(Repeat for each child.)

Part Four – Rationales
● **Ask children for rationales for using skill.**
"Why do you think it is important to _____?"

Part Five – Reality Check
● **Lead children through reality check.**
"Sometimes you might try really hard to _____, and this might happen." (Role play scripted example.)
"You just did everything right to _____. What should you do if this happens to you?"

Memorizing the Skill Lesson Format, with its lead-in sentences (see Activities 31 and 32), allows the presentation of the lesson to be automatic. If you are not concentrating on reading or remembering the lesson, you are free to enhance the introduction of the skill with even more valuable teaching. "Classroom survival skills," including paying attention, appropriate assertiveness, sitting still, keeping hands to self, and raising hands to speak (basic to a child's ability to "keep out of trouble" in the classroom), may be taught during the lesson presentation if you are constantly aware of opportunities to use the Teaching Strategies with these behaviors. On the other hand, if you read the lesson, you will find it more difficult to maintain your appearance of confidence and the smooth pacing that would keep the children's attention. You will also miss valuable opportunities to help children improve ongoing behavior.

Activity 31. Memorizing the Skill Lesson Format

At this point, memorize the italicized lead-in statements from the Skill Lesson Format.

Activity 32. Skill Lesson Format Quiz and Role Play

Give yourself a quiz by writing the italicized lead-in statements from the Skill Lesson Format verbatim from memory on a blank piece of paper. Compare your sheet with the format and study it further if there were any weak areas. Then, look over one or two actual skill lessons and practice role playing with your partner. Take turns being Teacher 1 and presenting the entire lesson, replacing child responses with pauses. Teacher 2 will have relatively little dialogue and can be responsible for providing Teacher 1 with feedback.

Preparing to Teach a Skill Lesson

Once you have memorized the format, you may prepare to teach a new skill by briefly going over the skill lesson and practicing the right way, wrong way, and reality check role plays. Somewhat more energy may be required to prepare children's role plays. Whenever possible, role play situations should "hit home." A sheet of possible role plays is provided for each skill; these are located behind each session outline in *Skill Lessons and Activities*. These role plays are designed to give the children a chance to practice the day's skill in situations relevant to their presenting problems, that is, their target behaviors. For example, during the lesson on Skill 6: Interrupting a Conversation, a child who typically has problems getting along with siblings and whose target behavior is "listening" might benefit from role playing the situation circled on the sample sheet of role plays on the following page.

The suggested role plays are categorized according to typical, recurring problem situations (top vertical column), and behavior problem types (left horizontal column). We have combined compatible target behaviors to form the seven categories of problem behavior. This, of course, does not imply that children may be easily typecast. It does share with you our experience with many personalities and recurring behavior problems. So, in order to provide an appropriate role play for *each* child in your group (or selected children in your classroom), first consider the individual child's target behaviors and situations; then choose an appropriate role play from the sheet or make one up to pertain to the child's behavior and the skill being taught. If you are working with other populations such as retarded adults, you can easily modify the role plays to make them relevant in terms of situation and age-appropriateness.

If you decide to create your own role play, be sure to make it simple, specific, and short; be careful to stick to the lesson at hand and avoid "hidden agendas" which might imply additional skills to be learned. For example, a role play can easily be made too complex by describing a situation involving several concerns. That is, role plays should not include other elements that might also legitimately be responded to. This role play for Following Directions is problematic:

Your mother tells you to clean your room right now. Your bus leaves for school in 5 minutes.

Following Directions (Skill 2) involves a pleasant face and voice, eye contact, a response of "OK," immediate compliance with the request, and satisfactory performance. The problem of missing the school bus implies that the child needs to either comply and miss the bus

Skill 6: Interrupting a Conversation
Role Plays

Situations Target Behaviors	School Problems (Teacher/Peers)	Neighborhood Problems	Sibling Problems	Parent Problems
Listen Carefully	Your teacher is giving the homework assignment to the class. You want to tell her that she forgot to hand out books.	Your two neighbor friends are explaining the rules of a game to you. You need to tell them that you can't play today.	Your older sister begins explaining a math problem to you. There's someone on the phone for her.	Your dad is giving you a list of chores to do. You notice that the dog is digging in the flower garden.
Treat Others Nicely	Two kids are talking in the doorway. You want to get out to recess right away.	Your friends are talking about a swimming class. You want to share some ice cream with them.	Your brothers are complaining that they have nothing to do. You just learned a new game you could teach them.	Your two little cousins are outside talking. Your dad tells you to invite them inside for a soda.
Join in with Others	Two classmates are talking about a movie. You need to tell one that the principal wants to see him.	Your friends are talking about a game they played yesterday. You want to suggest that you all play it right now.	Your older sister and brother are talking about which pizza parlor to go to. You want to suggest a different place.	Your parents are deciding where to go for a vacation this year. You want to suggest Disneyland.
Keep a Good Attitude	Two classmates are bragging about how well they can spell. You can't spell well, but you need a partner for a game.	Your friend's mom is explaining how to make doughnuts. But you already know how.	Your sister has been on the phone for a long time. You want to ask her where the toys are she borrowed from you.	Your parents are deciding against buying the bike you want. You want to suggest a skateboard instead.
Take Responsibility for Self	Your teacher checks your work and excuses you to recess. You need to tell her that you aren't finished, but she is talking.	The neighbors are complimenting you on how well you mowed the lawn. Your brother actually did it.	Your older sister is explaining a new game to your brother. Your mom told you to call them to dinner.	Your parents are talking about raising your allowance. You need to tell them that *you*, not your brother, broke the T.V.
Stay Calm and Relaxed	Your teacher is talking to another student. You need to ask her about a hard math problem before you go home.	Your friends are about to leave for the pool. You want to ask your mom if you can go. She is talking to a friend.	You finished your chores, but your sisters haven't. They are talking. Mom said you can all go skating when chores are done.	Your mom is telling you what to buy at the store and you need to tell her that you lost the money she gave you.
Solve Problems	Your classmate is holding the red marker and talking to a friend. You need to use it before the recess bell rings.	Your neighbors are in the yard talking about the flowers. You notice that the sprinkler is flooding their lawn.	Your brothers put some bread in the toaster and began talking about their baseball game. You think the toast might burn.	Dad comes home and begins telling you what a hard day he had. You need to tell him that you broke a window with your Frisbee.

or find a way to avoid having to clean the room right away so that the bus is not missed (perhaps involving Skills 11, 13, and 15). In other words, the skill being addressed in the lesson needs to be given the focus during initial practice trials. Other complexities that make it more difficult for a child to use this skill (e.g., compliance when a parent makes an unfair request) should be avoided so that the basic skill is clear.

Other suggestions for successful role playing would include placement of role play partners in close proximity to one another, use of eye contact, and maintenance of a serious attitude throughout the role play vignette. For very young, low-functioning, withdrawn, or confused children the teacher may need to coach a role player by means of a verbal cue whispered into an ear or physical prompts (gently lifting a chin to facilitate eye contact) if necessary (see coaching in Chapter 4). If you are teaching with a partner, another helpful technique for working with this type of child would be to divide the group into two smaller groups for the child role play portion of the lesson, with one instructor in each.

Sequencing the Skills

As already mentioned, plans for teaching the 17 skills are found in *Skill Lessons and Activities*. They are numbered in the suggested order for use. While there is nothing sacred about this order, it is the one we have found to be most useful. Basic skills, such as Following Directions and Sending "I'm Interested" Messages, are established early. More sophisticated social skills are addressed later after children have mastered the more basic skills. With very young or lower-functioning children, you will need to judge whether the children are capable of mastering more sophisticated skills. You may want to use only the more basic skills or adapt later lessons for these children (see Session 15, Skill 15, Giving and Receiving a Suggestion for Improvement).

Using the Skill Lessons without a Second Teacher

What about the teacher or other practitioner who decides to use the program without the luxury of a partner? Is it impossible? No. If you need to use the program without a fellow teacher, you can do it in most cases. The program was originally developed as a highly controlled, small-group format, for especially difficult-to-manage children. It has been used in many other contexts since. If you are not having to deal with *particularly troublesome* children, there is no reason that you cannot teach the skills without another instructor.

There are several techniques we have found to work well in adapting the skill lessons for one teacher. One easy technique with a number of advantages is the use of a child to play the part of Teacher 2 in the right-way, wrong-way, and reality check role plays. The privilege of helping the teacher may be awarded contingently to a child or children who have performed especially well earlier in the day. Children in the classroom who have completed their work quickly or made some substantial improvement on a target behavior could be picked for this privilege. A brief rehearsal before the skill lesson should be sufficient. Since the lessons are designed so that Teacher 1 is responsible for demonstrating the instance or noninstance of the skill, the child playing Teacher 2 is only responsible for set-up statements and need not know anything about the skill in advance.

Another technique that would be particularly appropriate for young children is the use of puppets. A single teacher may role play, with a friendly puppet taking the part of Teacher 2. The puppet can become something of a group mascot. Children may also wish to role play with the puppet; sometimes younger children get over initial shyness more quickly with puppets.

Other Elements of the Session – Optional Activities

In using the skill lessons you will give each child a strong foundation for using the new skills. To ensure that the children will apply the new skills, you must focus on the skills and follow up by using the Teaching Strategies in real-life situations that are problematic or in contrived situations that provide similar social pressures. As you teach the skill lesson you will have opportunities to use the Teaching Strategies to strengthen certain skills, mainly listening, eye contact, following directions, keeping a calm body, and volunteering, which are important classroom survival skills. In order to help children generalize more sophisticated, interactional skills, you must provide opportunities for them to practice the skills. The optional activities are designed to make opportunities for further practice both of the day's lesson and of other core and target behaviors.

If you have the opportunity to work with children in a natural setting, such as school or home, opportunities for practicing new skills should be numerous. Your task then will not be to create situations for practice, but to commit yourself to using existing situations to their fullest by deciding what behaviors you will be watching for and working on (see Chapter 3), and by using the Teaching Strategies to do so. If this describes your situation, read the rest of this chapter, carefully observing the treatment of the activities, i.e., how they provide for the utmost use of spontaneous interactions as social skills teaching episodes. Both the descriptions of the various optional components and the scripted session outline will provide you with specific information about skills to work on and examples of how to make the most of teaching opportunities.

If you do not have the advantage of working within a natural setting, or are interested in creating an even more intense social skills experience for the children, you may wish to use some or all of the optional activities to enhance the children's learning.

Using Homework

For every social skill lesson taught, there is a corresponding Homework assignment that requires the child to practice the skill at home or school and then write a short summary of the outcome. The purpose of giving assignments is to encourage the child to practice the skill in settings other than the contrived lesson situation. The child will, it is hoped, experience some social approval and be more likely to generalize the new behavior across all settings. For this reason, the Homework is an extremely important part of the acquisition of social skills.

When you make a new Homework assignment, you may want to read the exercises aloud to the group to make sure everyone understands what is expected. Encourage the children to ask their parents, siblings, or friends for help with the Homework exercises, if necessary. In the case of young children or others who for any reason cannot respond in writing to the questions, encourage them to get their parents or other helper to write the answers they dictate. You may want to hand out Homework at the end of the skill lesson or at the end of the group session. (See sample session outline at the end of this chapter.) An example of completed Homework for Skill 2: Following Directions appears on the following page.

Contingent use. Before the beginning of each lesson (except the first), you can ask the children for their Homework and quickly check it for quality. Children who have satisfactorily completed the Homework can enjoy a short reinforcing activity (such as free play time), while those children who have not satisfactorily completed the Homework can sit and complete it. You may gather the children into a group for collection of Homework (and the bottom half of the Home Notes, which are discussed later in this chapter) and then dismiss each one to free play or practice. Or, you may collect the papers from each child as he enters and then dismiss each one individually to free play or practice.

The Homework completion segment sets the stage for teaching and practicing several behaviors. Since the task of completing the Homework is less preferred than free play, it is a good time to watch for following directions. It is the child's responsibility to bring the Homework completed; this is a good time to watch and prompt for honesty (rather than excuse making or blaming others) and accepting consequences with a good attitude. Since some children have a problem remembering to bring or do their Homework, you can use the problem-solving sequence (Chapter 4) to work through some strategies for bringing it.

Free play offers many opportunities for the children to interact socially. It's a great time to practice joining in and other conversational skills, cooperation and patience for children who tend to take over or are bossy, problem solving, and following directions (see Instructions for Using Skill Lessons and Activities for a complete description of behaviors to watch for during the Homework completion/free play time).

Suggest to the children that if they do not get a chance to use the skill that week, they can write about what they would have done if they had had the chance to use it. When the session begins, give praise and Positive Feedback to children who brought completed Homework. Discuss selected Homework exercises in the group.

Progress chart. A Homework Progress Chart was used in demonstration groups to reinforce Homework completion (see example, p.72). Children bringing completed Homework were allowed to color in an entire Homework square or place a sticker on the square. Those children who satisfactorily completed their Homework during the free play were allowed to color in half of a square. On the last meeting of the group, a party was held, and those children having completed at least 80% of their Homework received a special prize (see party planning, Session 16).

The gift giving at the party worked as a motivator to encourage children to complete the bulk of their Homework assignments, while the free play times were more immediate motivation for the completion of weekly assignments. On occasion, children who were required to finish their Homework during free play in progress began to habitually bring their Homework to the group unfinished, expecting to finish it quickly and then join free play. The purpose of Homework is to encourage the practice of social skills in other settings and intensify the child's learning. To make up for these lost opportunities, children who habitually did not bring completed Homework were given more written questions and/or extra role play practice during the free play time. Remember, these children still got to color in half of a Homework square to work toward earning a gift on party day.

You may wish to adopt all or part of the Homework strategy used in the demonstration groups.

Using Relaxation Scripts

Each skill has a corresponding relaxation script to be used in the group session. In *Skill Lessons and Activities* there are eight scripts, which are designed to be used with more than one skill. The skills with which they are to be used are noted on the scripts themselves, and the appropriate relaxation script number is noted in each group session outline.

Skill 2: Following Directions
Homework

Name _Stephen R._

1. What are at least four things you can do to show that you are following directions the right way?

   a. _Look at the speaker_

   b. _and after the person is done say o.k._

   c. _and go do the thing that the person said right away_

   d. _____

2. Write down a direction your mom or dad gave to you. (What exactly did she or he say?) Then write down what you said and did.

   a. What did the other person say? _My mom said for me to go turn the water off_

   b. What did you say and do? _I said ok and I went and did it right away_

3. Write down a direction your teacher, babysitter, or some other adult gave to you. (What exactly did he or she say?) Then write down what you said and did.

   a. What did the other person say? _My babysitter said for me to go check the water_

   b. What did you say and do? _I said ok, went and did it_

4. What do you think you should do and/or say if someone gives you a direction, but you don't want to do it? (Tell why you answered this way.)

   a. What do you think you should do and/or say? _Do it anyway_

   b. Why? _If it's a grown-up, you need to._

Sample Homework Progress Chart

Nancy	Don	Lisa	Joe	Barb	Ed	Al	Meg
16	16	16	16	16	16	16	16
15	15	15	15	15	15	15	15
14	14	14	14	14	14	14	14
13	13	13	13	13	13	13	13
12	12	12	12	12	12	12	12
11	11	11	11	11	11	11	11
10	10	10	10	10	10	10	10
9	9	9	9	9	9	9	9
8	8	8	8	8	8	8	8
7	7	7	7	7	7	7	7
6	6	6	6	6	6	6	6
5	5	5	5	5	5	5	5
4	4	4	4	4	4	4	4
3	3	3	3	3	3	3	3
2	2	2	2	2	2	2	2
1	1	1	1	1	1	1	1

Each relaxation exercise lasts 7-10 minutes and is related to the specific lesson content for that day. The purpose of relaxation exercises is to teach the children to be aware of the differences between body tension and stress, and physical relaxation. Successful social interactions and learning are enhanced when the children can relax.

The relaxation scripts progress from teacher-guided tensing and relaxing exercises done in a prone position to more self-guided imagery in a sitting position. The intention is to teach the children some techniques for relaxing during actual social interactions.

There are two recurring themes in all of the relaxation exercises. First, the children are taught that when they are feeling tense, they can take a deep breath and expel it very slowly. Second, the children learn to use "positive self-talk." Positive self-talk is a positive self-statement thought to oneself. Our experience has taught us that one statement, used consistently, is easy for the children to remember and therefore is more likely to be used. The positive self-talk statement we use is, "I am calm."

You can read the relaxation scripts while playing soothing music in the background, or you may tape the scripts with music, and play them while you move about the room, giving the children some feedback on their relaxation efforts.

If certain children have trouble being relaxed in specific stressful situations, you may want to ad lib part of a relaxation session in order to talk directly about that real-life problem area. We have found that once the children are familiar with the relaxation techniques, they enjoy taking turns ad libbing parts of the training themselves.

In addition to practicing getting a calm body, the relaxation segment is a good time to watch for following directions and keeping hands to self.

Structuring Snack Time

Snack time is one of the ways of encouraging more natural social behavior. It serves the dual function of rewarding children who have participated appropriately during the lesson, while providing valuable teaching opportunities within an informal atmosphere.

We recommend that you make joining snack time contingent on the quality of effort and participation during the lesson. Choose those children who have done *especially* well during the lesson to perform the special jobs necessary in setting up for snack time. It is very important for you to specifically state those behaviors that have entitled these children to perform the special snack time jobs. This Positive Feedback reinforces those behaviors and communicates to the other children what behaviors are valued.

The children who have not initially earned snack time may earn the opportunity to join snack in progress by first practicing, to your satisfaction, those behaviors not mastered during the lesson. Position those children near the snack activity and ask them to practice alone such behaviors as sitting still and keeping their hands to themselves, or have them practice with you such behaviors as eye contact and volunteering. Always make sure the children know they have a chance to join the snack already in progress; as long as they are working toward something, they are less likely to misbehave.

Snack time is an excellent opportunity for the children to practice conversation skills, cooperation, and sharing (see Instructions for Using Skill Lessons and Activities for a more complete list). Its relative informality is conducive to the spontaneous peer interactions that are most valuable as teaching situations through the use of the Teaching Strategies, especially the Teaching Interaction and the Ignore-Attend-Praise sequence. Maximize the opportunities for using the Teaching Strategies. If the children tend to be shy and interact only with you, move away from the snack table until the children start interacting among themselves more. You may "float" in and out of close proximity to the snack table as needed. With a more verbal group, join the snack activity and take advantage of every opportunity to interrupt the spontaneous interactions that are not entirely appropriate. Use the Teaching Interaction to prompt the children to practice the more appropriate and/or complete behavior. Use Ignore-Attend-Praise to encourage those children behaving appropriately while prompting those children who are not behaving appropriately.

When snack time is over, ask all children to cooperate in cleanup. The cleanup phase of snack is a good time for you to watch for those children who are following directions and taking responsibility for specific chores. Because problems frequently will arise in transition times, the transition between one activity (snack time) and another (game time) will offer opportunities to use the Teaching Strategies to improve social behaviors.

The snack time strategy is equally, if not more, useful when working with other populations. Our experience with mildly retarded adult residents of a group home, for example, was that "refreshments" (perhaps wine and cheese in this case!) was an extremely relevant setting for the practice of social skills.

Using Activity Time

Another opportunity to create a more natural atmosphere is activity time. Each lesson is accompanied by a 20-minute activity designed to create a social atmosphere requiring the use of the social skills just taught. Because this part of the session is fun and seems less formal to the children, it encourages the spontaneous peer interactions that are important teaching opportunities. In most cases, children who were practicing during snack time will have rejoined the group and have the opportunity to benefit from activity time.

The activity sheets included in *Skill Lessons and Activities* point out the specific skills the activity is designed to promote; generally, activities provide for practice of such behaviors as cooperation, conversational skills, following directions, and problem solving (see Instructions for Using Skill Lessons and Activities for a more complete list).

Give the instructions and supply the materials (where necessary) for the day's activity. Then join the activity and take advantage of every opportunity to support desirable behaviors with praise and Positive Feedback, and interrupt undesirable behaviors with the appropriate Teaching Strategy.

Require the children to clean up after activity time. This cleanup period is another transition that offers opportunities to improve social behavior through the Teaching Strategies.

Using Home Notes

Schedule time near the end of the session to bring the children back into a group to fill out Home Notes as described here. During Home Note time, each child receives feedback and a written progress note or Home Note to take home. Each Home Note has a summary of the session's lesson, the skills taught, and an area for each child's individually identified behaviors, along with a portion for parent home observation and response. (See the completed Home Note for Skill 2: Following Directions.)

The Home Notes serve several important functions. First, they keep the parents aware of their child's progress, and they provide a summary of the skills taught. The parents are asked to watch for the use of new skills at home and respond on the bottom of the Home Note. This encourages the child to try the new behaviors in the home setting, and the parents to watch for and support new behaviors. When the child returns the parents' response to you, be sure to praise and encourage the child's efforts. Second, when the Home Note is filled out with the child, that child receives valuable feedback and review on her efforts for the day.

To facilitate efficient use of the Home Notes during the group time, prepare some sections ahead of time.

Skill 2: Following Directions
Home Note

Name __Stephen__   Instructors __Nancy + Cathy__

During today's lesson we practiced following a clearly given direction immediately after it was given and doing it with a good attitude.

Today's Objectives			**Target Behaviors**	
To follow directions, did the child:				Score
	YES	NO	A. _follow directions_	3
1. Use a pleasant face and voice?	✓	___	B. _ask, not tell_	2
2. Look at the person giving the directions?	✓	___	C. _say nice things_	1
3. Say "OK"?	✓	___	D. _good listener_	2
4. Start to do what was asked right away?	✓	___	E. _good attitude_	2
5. Do it satisfactorily?	✓	___		

Score, using this scale:
1 = Completely satisfied
2 = Satisfied
3 = Slightly satisfied
4 = Neither satisfied nor dissatisfied
5 = Slightly dissatisfied
6 = Dissatisfied
7 = Completely dissatisfied

The best thing your child did today in social skills was _looked at speaker, said nice things to others_

Parents – Please Complete This Section and Return
Skill 2: Following Directions

Name _____

The following objectives and target behaviors refer to those named above. Please mark or score your child in these areas and have him/her return this bottom section with your signature to the next social skills group.

Did your child meet the objectives of today's lesson at least once this week?			Score your child on his/her target behaviors, using the 1-7 scale above:
	YES	NO	
Objective 1	___	___	Target Behavior A _____
Objective 2	___	___	Target Behavior B _____
Objective 3	___	___	Target Behavior C _____
Objective 4	___	___	Target Behavior D _____
Objective 5	___	___	Target Behavior E _____

Parent Signature _____ Date _____

Fill out the demographic data and use the Target Behavior Worksheet to fill out the lists of the children's target behaviors on the Home Notes. This will allow you and your partner to focus on how each child is progressing. If a child seems to have mastered a skill, you may want to delete it and add a more refined skill.

When scoring the Home Notes in the small-group format, each teacher meets with half the group. Choose one child and ask the others to give some Positive Feedback to that child regarding her efforts during the session. While the feedback is being given, score the Home Note. Then ask the child to make some true and positive self-statements. Give the child some Positive Feedback, suggestions for improvement, and a copy of the Home Note. After the Home Note session is completed, you can excuse the children to go home if you've already handed out Homework.

The Home Note session encourages children to be aware of peer behavior and recognize positive and negative components. Children also learn to give and receive Positive Feedback and to make positive self-statements. (See Instructions for Using Skill Lessons and Activities for a more complete list of behaviors to work on.) For these reasons, it can be one of the most valuable teaching settings in the session.

Session Outline

The session outline combines the skill lesson with the optional activities in a scripted form based on the small-group 2-hour format. It draws together many of the suggestions from the previous chapters and applies them in a dialogue example. Use the session outline as a model for the dialogue you use for starting each activity and smoothly managing transitions between activities. We do not intend that you read or memorize the dialogue (with the exception of the skill lesson itself); however, you will find the program easier to use if you carefully study and imitate the sample dialogue. The session outline also points out which core and target behaviors are especially relevant to the activity.

If you have chosen a schedule different from the 2-hour demonstration model reflected here, you will need to concern yourself with a number of issues to effectively use the session outline. These include: (1) which of the activities you will be using; (2) in what order you will arrange them; and (3) whether they will occur consecutively within a block of time or be separated by other activities, e.g., other school subjects, recess, etc.

If you choose to substitute naturally occurring activities for some or all optional activites, keep the following in mind:

1. The skill lesson is intended to be followed by a fun (reinforcing) activity which is contingent on performance during the lesson. If you do not follow the lesson with snack time or some other reinforcing activity, you may lose important motivation. If you use an activity other than snack time, use the sequence for dismissing children to the snack table as a guide for structuring the transition to that activity.

2. Note that the first part of snack time is actually dismissing the children to the snack table. You will need to begin doing this just as the preceding activity ends. If you are not following the lesson immediately with snack time, you will need to use the dismissing procedure in whatever activity precedes it.

3. The other activities are basically self-contained.

4. Each activity in the session outline lists the core and target behaviors you will most likely have opportunities to work on at these times. If you are omitting an optional activity because you have a natural setting, make sure you plan for opportunities to work on all of the behaviors listed.

Note that new material only occurs in the skill lesson section, which is set in two columns. New informaion appears in regular type; the lead-in phrases to be memorized are in italic. Once you have read the first two session outlines, you will have very little new material to attend to.

The session outline for Skill 2: Following Directions is included here so that you can see at a glance how the skill lesson and optional activities can fit together, as we have recommended in this chapter.

Session 2

Skill 2: Following Directions

YOU MAY SUBSTITUTE naturally occurring events (lunch time, art projects, etc.) for items marked with an asterisk. Be sure to incidentally teach the day's skill, target behaviors, and the behaviors listed whether you use these activities or others. Remember that the dialogue provided in the session outlines (except for the lesson itself) is intended to be a model, not read or memorized verbatim. Read the dialogue over for main points and use your own spontaneous style. **Most of the dialogue and instructions are identical from skill to skill. For efficiency you may wish to attend only to the Relaxation Script number and the new information in the Skill Lesson.**

---

*Homework Completion and Free Play

In addition to today's skill and children's individual target behaviors, give special attention to taking responsibility, solving problems, and following directions (during Homework completion), and joining in, cooperating, problem solving, keeping a good attitude, and following directions (during free play).

Collect Homework and the bottom half of Home Notes; oversee free play and Homework completion or practice time.

Teacher 1:
(Scan papers to see which children have satisfactorily completed Homework; put aside Home Notes to check later.)

(children who completed it), you may go now and choose a game to play. (children who have not completed it), it's time for you to finish the Homework (or practice the skill) so that you can join the others.

(For children who habitually do not bring completed Homework, add more written questions or role play practice so that they finish about the same time as free play ends.)

Review Homework with children.

Teacher 1:
(Have children form a circle on the floor.)

Now let's look at the Homework you have done. I'm glad that (children who brought completed work) did their work at home. (a child who brought it), will you read your answer to Question _____?

(Have several children who brought their work read answers; ask for feedback from others. If you are using the Homework Progress Chart, allow children to color in the whole square or place a sticker in the square or color in part of it, depending on whether they brought completed Homework or finished it during free play.)

---

*Relaxation Training

In addition to today's skill and children's individual target behaviors, give special attention to keeping a calm body, solving problems, following directions, and keeping hands to self.

Lead relaxation training.

Teacher 1:
We are going to practice relaxing again. Relaxing will help you learn the new skill and help you face any problem.

(Have children find a place on the floor to lie down. Choose one child to turn off the lights.)

(Use Relaxation Script 1.)

Skill Lesson 2

● **Introduce skill and list components.**

Teacher 1:

Today we are going to talk about following directions. To follow directions, you:
- Use a pleasant face and voice.
- Look at the person giving the directions.
- Say "OK."
- Start to do what was asked right away.
- Do it satisfactorily.

. . . .

● **Role play appropriate example.**

Teacher 1:

This is the right way to follow directions. I'm at school, and my teacher is about to give me some directions.

Teacher 2:

_____, you need to throw your gum away.

Teacher 1:

OK. (gets up right away and throws gum away)

● **Ask children for behavior components of skill.**

Teacher 1:

How did you know that was the right way to follow directions?
(children respond or are prompted)

● **Role play inappropriate example.**

Teacher 1:

This is the wrong way to follow directions. I'm at school, and my teacher is about to give me some directions.

Teacher 2:

_____, you need to throw your gum away.

Teacher 1:

OK. (no eye contact, does not throw gum away; continues what he/she is doing)

● **Ask children for behavior components of skill.**

Teacher 1:

What should have happened to make that the right way to follow directions?
(children respond or are prompted)

. . . .

● **Ask children to role play.**

Teacher 1:

Now it is your turn to role play. (Assign role play situation.) I am going to call on someone who has been working really hard in the group by (specific on-task behaviors).

_____ has been working really hard the whole time by (appropriate behaviors) and looks ready to be the first one to role play. _____, this is your role play.

(Describe the role play you have previously selected for this child from the role play sheet behind this session outline. Have each child role play the skill *correctly* at least one time.)

● **Ask children to give Positive Feedback.**

Teacher 1 or 2:

Good role playing. Who can give _____ *some Positive Feedback on his/her role play?*

(Call on child who is volunteering and paying attention.)

. . . .

● **Ask children for rationales for using skill.**

Teacher 1:

Why do you think it is important to follow directions?
(children respond or are prompted)

Children:
- Makes you feel good.
- Helps you earn privileges.
- Keeps you out of trouble.
- Teachers and parents know you are listening.

. . . .

● **Lead children through reality check.**

Teacher 1:

Sometimes you might try really hard to follow directions, *and this might happen.* I'm at school, and my teacher is about to give me some directions.

Teacher 2:

_____, you need to throw your gum away.

Teacher 1:

OK. (gets up right away and throws gum away)

Teacher 2:

It's about time you followed my directions!

Teacher 1:

You just did everything right to follow directions. *What should you do if this happens to you?*
(children respond or are prompted)

Children:
- Take a deep breath to get calm.
- Keep a good attitude.
- Feel good about what you did.
- Keep trying.
- Make sure you follow directions right away every time.

*Snack Time

In addition to today's skill and children's individual target behaviors, give special attention to following group rules, using conversation skills, cooperating, and solving problems.

Decide which children have earned all of snack.

Children may earn the entire snack or only a smaller portion if they join the snack in progress. Keep in mind how much difficulty a child has had following rules or practicing during the lesson and relaxation time to get an idea of how much time the child might need to practice to compensate for missed opportunities.

Dismiss children who have already earned snack time to the snack table.

Teacher 1:
OK, it's snack time now. (Teacher 2), who do you think has really been earning snack today?

Teacher 2:
Well, _____ has been really following the rules, having a still body, volunteering, and working on (his/her target behavior).

Teacher 1:
Yes, he/she really has. And I think _____ has also done a really good job of (specific behaviors). I'd like (child already named) to go to the snack table and pass out the napkins and (other child named) to go and pass out the cups.

(Continue dismissing children to the snack table by giving Positive Feedback for their accomplishments and assigning them a task at the snack table. If some children have not earned all of snack, have them practice as follows.)

Teacher 1:
_____, you need to sit here with me and practice (volunteering, keeping hands to self, etc.).

(Ask children questions from the lesson, have them role play, or do relaxation to give them opportunities to practice behaviors that were problematic during relaxation and/or the lesson. As the children practice, watch for a good attitude and effort in practicing and determine when each child seems to have made up for lost opportunities and achieved an acceptable level of competence in the skill or rule following.)

Ask children to clean up snack area.

Teacher 1:
OK, snack time is over now. We need to clean up. _____, would you get the garbage can and bring it around so everyone can throw away the garbage.

(Use Positive Feedback and other Teaching Strategies for cooperating and following directions during the cleanup.)

---

*Activity Time

In addition to today's skill and children's individual target behaviors, give special attention to following group rules, using conversation skills, cooperating, and solving problems.

Explain activity for today's lesson.

Teacher 1:
It's time for an activity now. Today we're going to (describe activity briefly). This is a time for us to practice our target behaviors and Following Directions.

(Use Activity.)

Ask all the children to help clean up.

Teacher 1:
Now it's time for everyone to help clean up.

(Use Positive Feedback and other Teaching Strategies to help children work well together on cleanup. After cleanup, prompt children to return to circle.)

---

*Home Notes

In addition to today's skill and children's individual target behaviors, give special attention to following group rules and saying nice things.

Divide children into two groups and work on scoring Home Notes.

Teacher 1:
(a child), we are going to talk about how you did during today's session. Who can give (that child) some Positive Feedback and tell him/her good things about how he/she did on (target behavior)?

(Score the top half of the Home Note while the children are giving Positive Feedback. Ask for specific feedback for each of the child's target behaviors and add to it with comments you want to make, pointing out progress and areas needing improvement.)

(same child), now what do you think was the best thing you did in group today?
(child responds or is prompted)

Teacher 1:
That's good.

(Add specific descriptions of strong points.)

You might also try to (suggestions for improvement). Here is your Home Note.

(Repeat sequence with each child.)

---

*New Homework

In addition to today's skill and children's individual target behaviors, give special attention to following group rules and saying nice things.

Pass out Homework.

Teacher 1:
Here is your Homework. Be sure to do it and bring it back next time. Let's see what it says.

(Read aloud.)

If you need help, ask your parents or some other adult in your home.

Chapter 6

Putting It All Together – Practice

If you have done the activities thus far and practiced the Teaching Strategies in your own setting according to the Homework assignments, you probably are beginning to feel comfortable with the individual elements of the program. Along with these feelings of accomplishment, however, you may be less confident about your ability to make everything work together in a group session. Maybe you're wondering if you will notice when Sarah interrupts, when Billy – that withdrawn child – finally raises his hand, and if you will remember to use the appropriate Teaching Strategies for both Sarah and Billy, as well as keep track of where you are in the skill lesson. In short, if you are uncertain about putting it all together, don't worry. Such feelings are natural at this stage of the training. This chapter will provide the structure for practice that you still need to feel confident about making all the elements work for you in the group setting.

Importance of Practice

Practice is the key. Practice in a nonthreatening environment can be very helpful. "Nonthreatening envi-ronments" may or may not be easy to come by, but we'd like to suggest that you try a "dry run" of your new skills on some supportive friends, family, and/or colleagues. The remainder of this chapter will help you prepare to do this Dry-Run Role Play.

Procedures for Practice

Activity 33 provides an outline for preparing for the Dry Run. The Instructions for Dry-Run Role Play provide a script for introducing the activity to your volunteers and specific guidelines for both teachers and volunteers. Individual Instruction Sheets provide volunteers with descriptions of the children they will be portraying, as well as specific assignments for their behavior during the role play. The Observer Checksheet is included to provide an observer with specific guidelines for providing you with relevant feedback. See the filled-out example of an Observer Checksheet.

Activity 33. Preparing for the Dry-Run Role Play

A. Selecting Volunteers
   1. Confer with your partner. Come up with a list of four to six "volunteers" who would be willing to donate about an hour to helping you. If you know someone from whom you and your partner would feel comfortable receiving feedback, ask that person to be your observer.
   2. Read over the Behavior-Type Description on the Individual Instruction Sheets. Do not read the Role Play Description section on the Individual Instruction Sheets because that would let you in on the specific behaviors to expect from the volunteers during the Dry Run. You will get better practice by not knowing exactly what they will be doing.
   3. Assign behavior types to your volunteers, based on your knowledge of them. (Assigning a talking-out type to a volunteer who is typically the life of the party may be something you'll regret. Adults are notorious for overplaying kids' behaviors. Give yourself a break by picking volunteers who don't want to ad lib.)
B. Preparing Yourself
   1. Review Chapter 5, Introducing and Practicing New Skills.
   2. Look over the Instructions for Dry-Run Role Play in the present chapter.
   3. Read and rehearse the skill lesson and snack time procedures in a session outline in the *Skill Lessons and Activities*. We suggest you use Skill 2: Following Directions; it is fairly simple. Follow the procedure outlined in Instructions for Dry-Run Role Play.
C. Preparing Materials
   You will need:
   1. Instructions for Dry-Run Role Play.

2. Name badges.
3. Individual Instruction Sheets. (Make extra copies of the one for Model Child if you have more than one person to play that part.)
4. The skill lesson and snack time portions of the session outline you are going to use.
D. Planning Logistics
1. Develop a plan for contacting the volunteers.
2. Schedule the time and place of the meeting.
   a. Allow about 1 hour for the meeting.
   b. Select a carpeted room with at least 8 x 8 feet of empty space and a table with chairs for snack time.

Instructions for Dry-Run Role Play

Preparing for the Dry Run

Before meeting with the volunteers, complete the following tasks:
1. Review the Skill Lesson Format (Chapter 5); you should know this from memory.
2. From the skill lesson:
   a. Memorize the components for the day's skill.
   b. Memorize the situation for the right way, wrong way, and reality check role plays.
   c. Select several role plays for "children" in the group. Use the name badges to help you choose role plays that are appropriate for the child's target behaviors. If you wish, make up reminder cards to help you remember the role play situations.
3. Make extra copies of the Individual Instruction Sheets if you will need them. Cut out name badges and get pins or paper clips for fastening them.

Procedure for Conducting the Dry Run

At the meeting with the volunteers, do the following things:
1. If the volunteers are unfamiliar with the program, use the following dialogue to introduce the activity. If the volunteers are also being trained in the program, you may skip to Step 2.

   "This activity is a part of our training in the use of a program for teaching social skills to children. The program includes a format for presenting new skills which we will be using in this exercise. The program also specifies Teaching Strategies, which are interactions teachers use to instruct and support new social behavior as it occurs spontaneously. We will be using these Strategies in our interactions with you as you behave according to your instruction sheets. We ask that you carefully follow the instructions and avoid 'ad libbing.' When we respond to your behavior, you should be compliant with our requests.

   "You should be familiar with the rules of the group. The children know that the rules of the group include:

   a. I follow directions.
   b. I keep my hands to myself.
   c. I keep a good attitude.
   d. I look at the speaker.
   e. I raise my hand with a quiet mouth.

   In addition, they know that they will receive Positive Feedback and earn snack time by following the rules and participating in role play and discussion. They know that if they have trouble following the rules, a procedure called Sit and Watch may be used. This procedure involves removing the child to the periphery of the group for a short time. The procedure is demonstrated to the children during the first group session."

2. Pass out badges and instruction sheets to volunteers.
3. Go over each child's behavior type in the following way:
   a. Have each volunteer fill in his/her own name on the name badge and put it on.
   b. Starting with Child 1, have each volunteer read the Behavior-Type Description at the top of the Instruc-

tion Sheet. Have the volunteer illustrate the child's behaviors by role playing briefly for the group the kinds of behavior typical of the child.

4. Discuss the following guidelines for all volunteers:
   a. Each volunteer has three specific instructions to follow. Volunteers should respond appropriately at all times by looking at the speaker, sitting still, volunteering, and answering questions unless their specific instructions indicate otherwise.
   b. Volunteers should respond to the teachers' prompts.
   c. Volunteers should avoid engaging in "adult" behaviors, i.e., stepping out of role to comment about the process or their reactions to it.
5. Have volunteers study their parts for 3-5 minutes.
6. Form a circle on the floor, arranging volunteers to allow you the best use of physical prompts.
7. Role play. Teach the skill lesson, dismiss to the snack table, and begin snack time.
8. Stop the role play and discuss what happened. Share feedback for each person's performance and especially encourage volunteers to give feedback to teachers. Feedback from an observer may be shared now or later.

Name Badges for Dry-Run Role Play

CHILD 1   (real name)

Target Behaviors
   Ask, not tell.
   Show a good attitude.
   Follow directions.
   Raise hand with a quiet mouth.

CHILD 2   (real name)

Target Behaviors
   Volunteer
   Speak in an audible tone of voice.
   Look at the speaker.
   Join in at snack time.

CHILD 3   (real name)

Target Behaviors
   Keep hands and body still.
   Follow directions.
   Look at the speaker.
   Give on-topic answers.

MODEL CHILD   (real name)

Target Behaviors
   Follow directions.
   Show a good attitude.
   Look at the speaker.

Individual Instruction Sheet

Dry-Run Role Play Instructions for Child 1

Behavior-Type Description

    Child 1 is described as "verbally aggressive." This child typically talks out in class and bosses other children on the playground at school. The teacher complains that the child is "belligerent"; the child argues and pouts when corrected.

    The target behaviors identified for this child are:

— Ask, not tell.
— Show a good attitude.
— Follow directions.
— Raise hand with a quiet mouth.

Role Play Description
1. Raise hand saying, "Oh, I know, I know" for one of the first questions. Continue this each time a question is asked until the teacher praises other children for quietly raising hands or until he/she says you need to have a quiet mouth. Then raise your hand quietly to answer questions.
2. Sigh, frown, and mumble, "You never call on me" at some point when you volunteer, but the teacher does not call on you.
3. When you go to the snack table, tell another child how to do his job, i.e., take over.

Individual Instruction Sheet

Dry-Run Role Play Instructions for Child 2

Behavior-Type Description

    Child 2 has been described as "withdrawn." This child typically does not volunteer in class and is quiet and almost unnoticeable in the classroom. The child does not initiate interactions with others and tends to spend most of the time in solitary activities such as reading and drawing. When asked a question in class or when meeting new people, the child tends to blush and answer quietly.

    The target behaviors identified for this child are:

— Volunteer.
— Speak in an audible tone of voice.
— Look at the speaker.
— Join in at snack time.

Role Play Description
1. Look down and do not volunteer unless the teacher prompts you or praises other children for volunteering and looking at the speaker. If he/she does, improve your volunteering and looking at the speaker *gradually*.
2. Answer in a very quiet tone of voice. Continue to do so unless the teacher prompts you to have a louder voice.
3. When you go to the snack table, sit somewhat apart from the other children and do not join the conversation unless prompted to do so (prompts can take the form of direct instructions, teachers asking you to practice, or teachers contriving a reward for joining in).

Individual Instruction Sheet

Dry-Run Role Play Instructions for Child 3

Behavior-Type Description

Child 3 has been described as "hyperactive." This child is highly distractible, has a "short attention span," and seems to be in constant motion. The child does not typically complete tasks and often seems to be "in another world." The child appears not to be listening, giving "off-the-wall" answers to questions asked.

The target behaviors identified for this child are:

— Keep hands and body still.
— Follow directions.
— Look at the speaker.
— Give on-topic answers.

Role Play Description
1. Play with your shoestrings, watch, or other article of clothing. Continue to do so throughout the lesson unless the teacher praises other children for keeping "still bodies" or prompts you to get still. If he/she does, *gradually* improve your sitting still, responding to each prompt by keeping still for longer periods of time.
2. When called on to answer a question, say, "Is it snack time yet?"
3. When answering a question (with a correct answer), look away from the person to whom you are speaking.

Individual Instruction Sheet

Dry-Run Role Play Instructions for Model Child

Behavior-Type Description

The model child exhibits very few problem behaviors. In spite of referring problems, the child is very anxious to please and earn snack time today, so he/she does very well on the target behaviors.

The target behaviors identified for this child are:

— Follow directions.
— Show a good attitude.
— Look at the speaker.

Role Play Description
1. Volunteer for every question asked.
2. Look at the speaker almost all of the time.
3. Keep hands and body still.

Observer Checksheet

Directions: Use this form to record your observations of teachers during the Dry-Run Role Play. The list on the left indicates behaviors the teachers should be working on with each child. The columns across the top of the page describe responses the teachers might use. Each time a teacher responds to a behavior, write the teacher's initial in the appropriate column across from the child's behavior that was responded to. The program teaches instructors to praise children who are on task to help remind children who are *not* about what they should be doing. If certain children are not following rules (wiggling, looking away, etc.), the teacher may praise children who *are* following rules. When this happens you can record it in the "praise others" category next to the *off-task* child's name.

There is an additional blank row on the Checksheet for each child. It should be used to record any behavior that was not originally targeted but that the teachers responded to during the session. Use the "Other" column to record responses not covered by the categories on the page. Do not record lesson dialogue or other comments that do not relate to child behavior.

Observer Checksheet

Teacher Responses Child Behavior	Praises Child	Praises Others	Prompts	No Response	Other
Child 1 _____ (fill in real name)					
Ask, not tell					
Show a good attitude (does not frown or mumble)					
Follow directions					
Quiet mouth/raising hand without speaking					
Child 2 _____ (fill in real name)					
Volunteer					
Speak in an audible tone of voice					
Use eye contact (look at the speaker)					
Join in (at snack time)					
Child 3 _____ (fill in real name)					
Keep hands and body still					
Follow directions					
Use eye contact (look at the speaker)					
Give on-topic answers					
Model Child _____ (fill in real name)					
Follow directions					
Show a good attitude (Use a pleasant face and voice)					
Volunteer					
Keep hands and body still					
Look at the speaker					

Observer Checksheet

Teacher Responses / Child Behavior	Praises Child	Praises Others	Prompts	No Response	Other
Child 1 _Ann_ (fill in real name)					
Ask, not tell					
Show a good attitude (does not frown or mumble)				✓	
Follow directions					
Quiet mouth/raising hand without speaking	N N N V N	N N N V V N		✓	
Child 2 _Cathy_ (fill in real name)					
Volunteer	N N V N				
Speak in an audible tone of voice	N				V Teaching int.
Use eye contact (look at the speaker)	N V N N N N		N N V		
Join in (at snack time)					
Child 3 _Joyce_ (fill in real name)					
Keep hands and body still	N V	N N			N N V V
Follow directions					
Use eye contact (look at the speaker)	V N N	N V			N V
Give on-topic answers	N	V N			N N
Volunteer	N N N	N			N
Model Child _Candy_ (fill in real name)					
Follow directions					
Show a good attitude (Use a pleasant face and voice)					
Volunteer	N N V N				
Keep hands and body still	V				
Look at the speaker	N N N				

Chapter 7

Making It Work for You in Your Setting

Clarity about your social expectations and proficiency in the Teaching Strategies should allow you to turn any interactional situation into a social skills teaching episode. The skills you have learned thus far are the absolute essentials and should characterize your use of the program, regardless of your setting, the type of students you work with, or the resources you have. All uses of the program should have in common the systematic presentation of new skills through the skill introduction sequence (skill lesson) and consistent use of the Teaching Strategies. Beyond this, however, each user's adaptation will be unique, and will ensure that the program enhances the environment without disrupting it.

This chapter provides an in-depth description of factors to be considered in using small-group instruction and shares variations employed by users in other settings. Inherent in this discussion is the assumption that you are the best person to evaluate the needs and limitations of your setting and to design a format for using the program that is compatible with your needs. Therefore, we ask you to (1) carefully read the chapter, (2) consider your needs and limitations, (3) think of creative adaptations, and (4) use only what will enhance your use of the program.

Components from the Small-Group Format

The small-group format refers to the logistics and scheduling protocols employed in our demonstration groups. In this application, 6 to 8 children met with 2 instructors twice weekly for 17 sessions. As earlier indicated, each day's schedule allotted time for the following activities: contingent free play earned for completing the last session's Homework, Homework review in the group, relaxation training, the presentation of the skill lesson, snack time, activity time, and time for filling out Home Notes in a small group.

There are a number of pros and cons for using the small-group format. Children whose social problems are more severe may need the greater amount of individual attention available in a small group. The small group fosters more intimate relationships among children and closer monitoring and support for individual children. Practitioners including school counselors or psychologists, mental health professionals, or special education teachers who are likely to work with small groups of children and are usually responsible for more problematic children may wish to use the small-group format.

Using the small-group format involves solving a number of logistical concerns. Basically, these define the who, what, when, and where of the group.

Working as a Teaching Team

As stated earlier, it is very possible that you will be working alone as you teach the program. However, if you are considering using the small-group format and are working with "problem" children, you may want to have two instructors for the group. If you indeed are dealing with children whose problems are severe enough to be referred out of the classroom, two instructors can be a must. For each lesson, one person acts as a lead teacher (Teacher 1), taking responsibility for teaching the lesson and setting up role play vignettes for the children. The other person acts as a backup teacher (Teacher 2), helping to reinforce the concept of the lesson and adding comments and information as necessary. However, the most important function of the backup teacher is to praise the children who are attending, volunteering, giving on-topic answers, eye contact, etc. In addition, the backup teacher is responsible for dealing with misbehavior or lack of attending so that the lead teacher can present the lesson as smoothly as possible. It is helpful to alternate positions so that each instructor learns to teach the lessons and to act as backup.

There are a number of tricks to maximize the advantage of having two teachers. Some of the most important are physical positioning, nonverbal communication, and consistency through concurrence. If you arrange children so that they are always monitored by at least one teacher, you as teachers can maintain the illusion of having "eyes in the back of your heads." You can do this sitting across from each other in the group circle, having one of you move to the snack table with the children, and keeping your backs to the wall in other settings, as shown in the following drawings. It is helpful to place "difficult" children on either side of you so that you can easily use physical prompts and approval.

Nonverbal communication is vital to the pacing of the lesson. While both of you should constantly be scanning the group, you should be careful to catch one another's eyes frequently. This allows for interrupting appropriately to add to the lesson or to use Teaching

Strategies, and it may communicate such important messages as, "Yes, I agree Shawn may need to go to Sit and Watch. Keep an eye on him."

Agreement between you as teachers is an important way of establishing consistency. This can be encouraged if Teacher 1 says, "Wow, Angela is raising her hand a lot today – don't you think?" Teacher 2 agrees with Teacher 1's praise before going on with an additional comment. For example, Teacher 1 might say, "Thanks, Melinda, for keeping your hands to yourself," and Teacher 2 might add, "Yes, she's done really well with that today, and I also noticed that Jeremy is volunteering more." While you never argue or discredit each other in front of the children, one of you may contradict the other in some instances in the following manner:

Teacher 1:
Well I think Jim is ready to go to snack now.

Teacher 2:
Yes, Jim's been doing better on paying attention. But I think Susan *really* earned going to snack first because she volunteered almost every time today!

Planning for Physical Space

The program has been taught in a variety of surroundings, from tiny, cramped rooms to spacious, carpeted classrooms. In selecting the location for the group, you should consider the functions of furniture and space. If you and the children sit in a circle on the floor, the atmosphere can be more relaxed and you can more carefully watch the children and each other. If you are in a classroom, simply move desks and chairs to the walls so that you have enough space. If the floor is not carpeted, you may be more comfortable with everyone sitting on chairs in a circle. Innovative instructors have compensated for less comfortable rooms by using pillows, carpet squares, and folding chairs. When considering the space you will be working with, keep in mind that you will need enough room for the children in the group to stretch out full length on the floor for relaxation training (if you're using it). There should be enough room so that children are not in contact with each other, furniture, or the walls.

Selecting Children

Identification. Evaluations of children who were involved in the demonstration project indicated that most children use more appropriate social skills after involvement in the group (see Chapter 1). Participation in the group is usually a successful, positive experience for children. Those children with certain interactional patterns, however, are most effectively treated by the program.

Skill-deficit model. The program assumes that the child does not have the behavioral repertoire to function effectively and positively in social situations. Thus, a child who is most appropriate for training does not exhibit positive social behaviors; the child may seem awkward and clumsy in situations that require interactions with peers and adults. Other children and adults may not like the child. Some may label the child's behavior as "aggressive," but acts of aggression usually occur as a result of others "picking" on the child, the child being called names, and/or the child acting in frustration in a problem setting.

Generally, children most appropriate for this training are those who lack the skills identified and taught in the curriculum and/or who can be described by the target behaviors listed in Chapter 3.

Not a panacea. Children who are frequently referred to as bullies and who can be quite socially appropriate "when they want to" may have problems that are motivational rather than based on a skill deficit. These children might learn new skills from this program or learn to use skills in new settings. However, these children and others with more involved problems may also need other, more intensive programs or therapy. While this program may not be expected to solve all of a child's problems, it might be an extremely functional addition to other approaches.

Process of screening. You may screen children for involvement in the program through subjective or more objective means.

Teachers have been shown to be reliable predictors of children's success in various situations (Greenwood, Walker, & Hops, 1977). If a teacher or counselor is very familiar with the children being considered for participation, professional judgment is probably a highly appropriate method of selection.

The foregoing discussion of who will benefit most should assist a teacher or counselor in selecting those children who would be most appropriate for this program's training.

In other situations, where the instructor is not familiar with the children eligible for involvement, or where justification for providing this extra service to some children and not others is needed, one or more of the screening procedures that follow may be desirable. These procedures may also be useful in program evaluations.

1. **The Louisville Behavior Checklist** (Miller, 1977). The Louisville Behavior Checklist is a standardized parent-report behavior checklist described in Chapter 1. During the second year of the demonstration project the data from Louisville Behavior Checklists were analyzed for the purpose of determining whether profiles from this instrument could be used to predict the appropriateness of a child for this program. This was done by comparing program instructors' judgments of a child's appropriateness to the child's prescores on the Louisville. Children were categorized by instructors as appropriate, marginally appropriate, or inappropriate because of competing problems. The results suggest that children who are judged appropriate for the program average about 1 standard deviation above the mean (60) on scales that relate to goals of the program (e.g., aggression, social withdrawal, etc.).

2. **The Consumer Satisfaction Scale** (Appendix A). This instrument is somewhat easier to use than the Louisville. It is not standardized, but it provides ratings on behaviors included in the program's 17 core skills. A child who is rated 3 (slightly dissatisfied) or lower (dissatisfied or completely dissatisfied) on eight or more items is a likely candidate for training.

3. **Other checklists and rating scales.** A variety of standardized measurement instruments are available for determining children's social adjustment to school and/or home settings. Any device that would identify children with deficits in the areas to be taught would probably be appropriate. Cartledge and Milburn (1980) provide a review of a number of scales and inventories that can be used with children.

4. **Behavioral observations.** Although difficult to obtain in some settings, observational records of actual incidents of problem behaviors make a simple and useful supplement to other screening processes. For example, you can make a tally of various social behaviors of concern, perhaps in the classroom and on the playground. This would provide a clear indication of the extent of the problem. If you see the child daily and will be providing social skills instruction in the same setting in which your observations of the child are made, this procedure would be especially recommended.

Grouping Children

The number of children involved in the group should be determined by considering the functioning level and age of the participants. Younger children or lower-functioning children will require more attention and will need more work in the basic areas such as attending. Thus, they will probably be more effectively treated in smaller groups. For example, the demonstration groups usually included 8 children; for 6- and 7-year-olds, however, groups were limited to 6 children. With a ratio of 6 to 8 children to 2 instructors, each child receives a high rate of praise and individual attention, and has many opportunities to role play and practice the new skills as well. During the lesson, snack time, and activity, the instructors are able to attend to and reinforce the behaviors being taught and to correct inappropriate behaviors. Another major advantage of the small-group format is the development of more intimate peer and teacher relationships.

Age-grouping helps ensure that children are with a realistic peer group, one whose approval will be important. We usually group first- and second-graders, third- and fourth-graders, and fifth- and sixth-graders. Occasionally, it might be advisable to group a child with children who comprise a peer group suggested by maturity and functioning level. For example, an exceptionally bright child who is big for her age might be grouped with children who are chronologically older. This decision might be reversed, however, if that child also had a problem with acting older or "superior" and was turning off her own peers. On the other hand, grouping immature children with younger children could have the advantage of ensuring the child greater success and acceptance than is possible with a same-aged peer group. You should exercise caution in this case, as well, to avoid strengthening the child's immature behavior with immature models.

While homogeneity with respect to age groups is desirable, heterogeneous mixtures of problem types should be sought. Children who are more aggressive should be grouped with those who are more withdrawn. Groups comprised entirely of aggressive children or withdrawn children will result in too much or too little behavior and, consequently, fewer teaching opportunities. It is also likely that combination of the two extremes will allow for some modeling, pulling both factions closer to the mean.

Choosing a Schedule

The temporal parameters (how often, how long, and at what time the group should meet) can be flexible. The demonstration model may provide you with a design for scheduling that you might wish to adopt, or it might simply be the starting place for you to explore considerations and come up with a plan that better meets your needs.

The demonstration groups met for 2 hours per session, twice per week, and lasted for 17 sessions. As mentioned previously, the project was located in a mental health center, physically distant from many of the children's natural environments; these factors created certain limits. Groups met for 2 hours to allow enough time for both presentation of the skill and all the optional activities, to compensate for not being in the child's natural environment. Meeting twice each week ensured some intensity; children were kept involved enough that they did not forget what they had learned. Since the mental health center was some distance from the children's schools, and since the children in a group came from several different schools, groups were held after school. In experimenting with different numbers of sessions, we found that children seemed to really start showing improvement after about 10 sessions. Earlier versions that ended after 11 sessions left the teachers feeling frustrated and saying, "If I only had a little more time with these kids." Lengthening the groups to 17 sessions seemed to allow children more adequate practice time and helped to stabilize new skills.

Adaptations of the program in other settings have demonstrated variations that do not seem to detract from its effectiveness. One school-based replication site scheduled groups right before lunch. They followed the same schedule for the group up until snack. Lunch (within the group setting) replaced snack time and activity time was dropped. Since lunch could not be made contingent, motivation was aided by having children practice while some children had special desserts and/or "early" lunch and subsequent early release to recess. Another school-based group was scheduled around recess, which was used as a contingent activity time. Some self-contained special classrooms (for emotionally handicapped children) scheduled groups as an activity within the classroom two or three times a week. The two teachers taught the lesson and followed it with a contingent snack. Other sites varied components such as holding groups once a week instead of twice, having fewer sessions, and having a group for 1 hour taught by a school psychologist. In a group home for retarded adults 1½-hour sessions were held twice weekly as soon as the residents came home from work. Refreshments (wine and cheese) were also appetizers prior to evening meal preparation.

Extent of Adaptations

A major concern of program developers is the extent to which program adoptions will resemble the original model and reflect the developers' intent. On one hand, it may be stated that only exact duplication will maintain the integrity of the program and its results. This of course assumes that all program components must be adopted in their original form. On the other hand, giving adopters a free rein may be desirable since their creative input will foster a sense of investment in the program and will result in greater use. In addition, local circumstances may be different, requiring modification of some procedures.

You may have noticed that a compromise between these two perspectives is suggested here. We urge you to adhere to (adopt) the core components which are basic to the success of the program. We invite you to reinterpret, enhance, rearrange, or delete (adapt) the optional components.

The core components and elements which are non-negotiable include: (1) commitment to positive interactions in general; (2) careful definition and clarification of behavioral expectations; (3) introduction of new skills according to the skill lesson in the session outlines so that experiences and practice are maximized; and (4) careful and consistent use of the Teaching Strategies to ensure that children interact positively and are supported for doing so.

It's true that we have become somewhat biased with respect to these basic elements. But then, they have been present in all the successful applications of the program but not in unsuccessful ones. Yet, we are not so wedded to our own ideas that we are blind to the many creative adaptations made by users. School counselors have shown us that groups can be taught in 1- to 1½-hour sessions built around recess or lunch and that running groups twice a week may not be easy or desirable within some school settings. Regular elementary school teachers have shown us that the Teaching Strategies make math and reading lessons run more orderly and smoothly. Numerous other counselors, psychologists, and teachers have played with scheduling and use of what we now call optional activities, repeatedly demonstrating that encouraging creativity in these areas is quite helpful and appropriate. Thus, we ask you to find creative ways of utilizing the four non-negotiable components. You should find them to be valuable tools in virtually any setting.

Involvement of Parents and Others

Depending upon your setting, you may want to involve some of the "important others" from the child's environment in the program experience. Whom you involve and the level of involvement may vary, depending upon your setting and the amount of time you wish to spend. For example, if you are a teacher in an elementary school, you may have easy access to other teachers or other school personnel who interact with the children you are teaching; or if you are a mental health professional, you may already have frequent contacts with the parents. If you are teaching in a small special education class, you may consider it reasonable to have a high level of involvement with other teachers and/or parents. On the other hand, very limited involvement may be more reasonable in a class of 30 children. This section is designed to describe some options for the types of contacts you might have with others. These progress from the least to most demanding levels.

Planning and Initial Assessment

The first major role of parents, teachers, and others is to provide you with information that will aid in the screening of children and the identification of behaviors (see earlier section of this chapter for the process for screening children). As already noted, screening devices such as the Louisville Behavior Checklist, the Consumer Satisfaction Scale, and verbal reports should also be used for initial goal setting. An Individual Education Plan (I.E.P.) may be written for each child as a cooperative effort by you, the parent, and other appropriate participants. This plan would specify the specific behavioral goals for the child and the means for measuring the child's level of functioning with respect to these goals before and after the training.

Making Progress Reports

The most basic level of involvement is informing parents and others about the child's experiences and progress in the program. The main vehicle for accomplishing this is the Home Note, designed to provide a fast, concise means of describing the child's experience and progress. It is probably the easiest way to provide information to parents or others who may wish to know what happens as the child is involved in the program. Reporting progress *during* training accomplishes a number of things. It allows parents and others to watch for and support new skill use by the children; it lets others compare their perceptions of the program to what it is actually doing; it provides some training to others as to what social skills are important to social adjustment; and it may increase others' support for the program as they become involved with it and begin to have a sense of commitment and "ownership."

Providing Two-Way Communication

Communication between you and others involved with the child may be accomplished in several ways. The Home Note provides a quick and easy way of sending information *back and forth*. Multiple carbons can be used if you want to send several copies, such as to parents, teachers, and others. Since the child sees these people daily, he can take responsibility for carrying the Home Note from place to place and obtaining feedback from various sources, returning the forms to you at the next meeting.

More personal contacts such as telephone calls may also be desirable. The demonstration groups included a system for phoning parents before, during, and after the group to obtain information about the child's behavior at home by asking them whether the child was using each of the 17 skills. That system provides valuable information about the child and an opportunity for interaction between you and the parent. Replications of the program in school settings did not use the phoning system.

Face-to-face contact between you and others may also be a valuable tool. If parents provide transportation for their children, you may talk to them when they come to pick up their child. If the program is conducted in a school, you can see other teachers in the hall or lounge; in a mental health center, you can easily contact other professionals familiar with the child.

Training Parents and Others

In some situations, especially with more difficult children, it may be desirable to train others to follow through with the work you are doing. This Guide may be used to train parents, teachers, and others, but it is important that you carefully weigh the benefits versus the expense of undertaking such training. The demonstration project did not always obtain better results when parents were also given training. However, if you are already in a position to train others (such as a mental health professional offering training in parenting), you may find this component an extremely desirable one.

We would suggest the following components for training parents or others to support a child's program experience:

1. Use Chapter 3 with minor adaptations to teach parents or others the essentials of clearly defining expectations for behavior and use Chapter 4 for teaching the Teaching Strategies to support improvements. Emphasize role playing and Homework.

2. If possible, have the parents observe you working with the child. It is desirable for observation to be

incognito through one-way glass, but this is rarely possible.

3. Observe the parents or others interacting with the children. Use the Teaching Interaction to help refine skills. At times parents might even join a group session to try using Teaching Strategies learned earlier in a parent group.

Practical Answers to Common Questions

You've been through all the elements of the program and considered adaptations for your own situation, but you may still be wondering if there aren't still some gaps somewhere.

While this Program Guide has been designed to inform you of every possible thing you might want to know about using the program, we realize that goal probably isn't realistic. In our experiences of training people to use the program, we have found that participants' questions do much to "fill in the gaps" and clarify the materials covered in training. Though we can't possibly recount all of the excellent questions we've been asked or anticipate ones that you might have, we would like to share some of the discussions that have occurred repeatedly during training.

When you use the Direct Prompt with a child, can you say "please"? When you are using any of the Teaching Strategies, it is important that you be consistent and sincere. If you feel that you need to make some *minor* changes in your delivery of the Teaching Strategies so that you will feel more comfortable with them, go ahead. However, they are written so specifically for a purpose: to ensure that all interactions that you have with the children help to improve their behavior and end positively. Make sure that the minor changes you make still preserve the intent of the Teaching Strategy and ensure positive closure with the children. The intent of a Direct Prompt is to specify how behavior should be corrected. In this sense, the Direct Prompt is not the same as giving directions. If you can say "please" without implying doubt or hesitation about your command, go ahead.

What do you do about a child who has a particular problem behavior with which you have tried everything, but nothing has worked? Frequently when people complain that they have "tried everything," that is just the problem. Carefully think about the different strategies and techniques that you have tried. Perhaps you did not persist long enough with a single strategy to get any results (changing behavior takes time); perhaps you were not consistent with the child; perhaps you have not been positive and calm in your approach to the child, causing you to lose credibility with her; perhaps the things in the environment avail-able as reinforcers are not interesting to the child; or perhaps your expectations of the child are not clear. If you don't get results, once you have explored these areas of possible problems, call in an objective person to help you problem solve.

What do you do when you've asked a child what she would do in a problem situation, and she answers that she would respond negatively in some way? In this situation you can use the problem-solving skill contained in the curriculum. Ask the child what the consequence of her suggested solution would be to her (invariably something negative). Then ask her to come up with at least two other possible solutions that would yield better personal consequences. If she cannot think of any, you suggest them. Do not deny that her natural inclination to respond negatively in a problem situation is warranted. The point to be learned here is to remain calm and think of several constructive solutions to a problem (see the problem-solving example that is found in Chapter 4).

What do you do if the process seems to disintegrate, i.e., if no one is behaving well (three children in Sit and Watch and no one earning snack)? Don't let this happen! The group process may begin to disintegrate for many different reasons. Perhaps your environment is not particularly reinforcing, or the lesson is going too slowly, or you are emphasizing the conceptual aspects of the lesson instead of the role playing, or you have neglected to start the session with lots of recognition for positive behaviors (especially being *ready* by looking at the speaker, having quiet mouths and still bodies). For these or other reasons you may find yourself with several off-task and disruptive children. And although no children may be behaving up to their potential, at any one given moment some will be behaving better than others. Choose those children who are behaving most positively (or least negatively) and give them some very special reinforcers. Let the other children know that they can earn these reinforcers too when they have met your very specific expectations for behavior. It is important to remain calm and positive. Evidence of frustration, resentment, and anger on your part will only cause the situation to disintegrate further. The goal is to get the children back on task so that they can continue to have a positive learning experience, not to punish.

What do you do when you try to use the Teaching Interaction during an argument over a game, but you just can't seem to get the children's attention away from the game? In order for the Teaching Interaction to be successful, you will need the children's complete attention. However, when a negative interaction is occurring in relation to a preferred activity, it is very difficult for you to draw the children's attention away from the activity and to yourself. In order to do this in a neutral way, simply remove the activity or an essential component of the activity without saying anything to the children. The removal of the activity allows the children to focus complete attention on you. After the children have responded appropriately to the Teaching Interaction and are exhibiting the "ready" behaviors, you replace those items that had been removed and the activity resumes. If there is a subsequent problem with the activity, discontinue it. A more detailed description of this technique can be found in Chapter 4.

What if a child does not respond to Positive Feedback? This is not a typical problem, but it does occasionally occur. If you are using Positive Feedback to strengthen behavior, you are assuming the child likes it when people give him personal attention and acknowledge what he has done. If the child does not respond to Positive Feedback, he is not reinforced by it. In such a case you will need to observe the child carefully to determine what types of experiences he finds desirable and reinforcing. You can then *pair* those experiences *with* Positive Feedback and then gradually fade them while continuing to use the Positive Feedback. We rely heavily on Positive Feedback as a reinforcer because it is readily available and easy to use.

Don't the children get used to having too much Positive Feedback? Do they use it as a crutch? We have not found this to be a problem even though data have shown that the children in our groups experience Positive Feedback from the instructors at a rate of about four times per minute. Giving and receiving Positive Feedback is part of the curriculum, and we are constantly modeling it for the children. Consequently, the children become quite adept at it themselves. We believe this makes them more reinforcing to be around and thereby improves their chances for more positive social interactions with peers and adults in their environment.

Do the program techniques work with shy children? We have experienced very positive results when working with shy or withdrawn children. If you create a warm, positive, and supportive environment, you can usually encourage the shy children to gradually take more and more risks and try new skills. It is important that these children experience success and approval for *any* efforts toward more appropriate behavior. Since shy children typically will not spontaneously try new behaviors, it is vital that you balance encouragement for trying new things with careful understanding of the children's limits and abilities so that they experience success.

Do children anticipate the role play part of the lesson and want you to hurry? We have found that once the children are used to role playing, most of them consider it to be fun and therefore probably prefer it to other parts of the lesson. Since role playing is a time for the children to be more actively involved in learning the new skill by actually practicing it, any preference for role playing is an asset. The more conceptual parts of the lesson are intentionally kept to a minimum, allowing the children more practice (role playing) time.

How do you individualize role plays for the children on the first day? If you do not personally know the children and have not had the benefit of observing them beforehand, you will have to rely on information about their needs from parents, teachers, and other sources. If you do not have any information, you will have to choose some role plays randomly from the lesson. After just a short time with the children, however, it should become obvious to you what their particular strengths and weaknesses are, thereby enabling you to individualize all future role plays for them.

Should you discuss children's feelings of anger when they are unsuccessful? When children are talking about or otherwise expressing feelings, we do not attempt to counsel them. Instead, we use this input as a vehicle for helping them to constructively solve their problems. Problem-solving techniques are a part of the curriculum, and feelings of anger, frustration, defeat, and sadness that children may express in relationship to their interactions with others are excellent real-life situations in which to practice these problem-solving techniques. We do not deny that in a particular situation the child may have wanted to react negatively or that the person she was interacting with may have deserved a negative reaction; instead, we help the child work out a solution that would benefit her in the most positive way possible.

What do you do if a child is anti-group? Most of the children that we have worked with have expressed positive feelings about the group. They find it to be a fun experience and are disappointed when the group is over. In order to be motivated to practice and learn new skills, children must find membership in the group to be comfortable and fun. If this is not the case with a particular child, you will need to try to determine what the problem is. The child my be embarrassed to role play, feel she doesn't fit in with the other children, or be bored. In some instances children are not accustomed to being in such a structured environment where there are so many expectations of them, and they may be resistant and noncompliant. If you can determine what the problem is, you may be able to take steps to make the child feel more positive toward the group. On occasion you may have a child in your group who is not really appropriate for the group. That is, her needs are not those that can be served by what the curriculum has to offer.

What if a child does not want to come to a group session? Once a child is a member of your group, it is vital that he come to every group session so that he will experience continuity in the curriculum, consistency in working on target behaviors, and familiarity with the other group members. When peers have formed a cohesive group, they will all feel more comfortable in trying new skills. Though some children may voice resistance to coming to a session, once they are involved they almost always enjoy experiencing success and peer and adult approval. Therefore, group members should not have the option of choosing whether or not to come to a particular group session. The parent or other adult who is responsible for getting the child to the group should bring the child regardless of complaints. Most children get "hooked in" after a few sessions. If not, examine other factors and consider alternate referrals. A child who persists in fighting involvement in the group is unlikely to benefit from it and may detract from the experiences of other children in the group.

What do you do about a child who has deep-seated emotional problems? If you believe that children's problems, "deep-seated" or otherwise, are manifested in their overt behavior, then you can work to improve those behaviors. When children can interact with their peers and adults more positively and experience social approval, there is a good chance that they will not be perceived as having such severe problems. If after working with a child you are concerned that she may be chronically depressed, unhealthy, etc., it is advisable to refer her to a resource with more expertise in determining and treating such problems.

What do you do when you have tried a particular Teaching Strategy and it didn't work? Two major reasons that a Teaching Strategy will not get desired results in a given situation are that you have used it incorrectly or it was not the appropriate Teaching Strategy to use in that situation. When a Strategy does not work, you need to rethink the situation, choose a more appropriate Strategy, and use it in a calm, positive, and confident way.

Sometimes I feel sorry for a child, and I want to "bend" the group rules to accommodate the child better. Is this OK? Sometimes it is very easy to get distracted by the occurrences of the moment and not be able to "see the forest for the trees." It is of utmost importance that you keep your long-term goals in mind; that is, judge situations by the impact they will have in the long run as well as immediately. What you are asking children to do *is* difficult. At times their difficulty may be demonstrated in frustration, anger, and even tears and sullenness, which may trigger your fears about your abilities to help them. The best way to deal with these situations is to determine your level of flexibility by the following criteria:

– If you feel like changing the rules because you feel sorry for the child, because you are afraid he won't like you anymore, or because you are just unsure of what to do, *don't!*
– If you feel like breaking the rules into smaller bits because you see ways for the child to be successful in smaller steps, *do* it!

This is why it is so important for you to remain consistent with rules you *believe* in; snap judgments, especially those involving all-or-nothing-type promises or threats, get you into great trouble.

A Final Word

If we have achieved our primary goal, we have provided you with ideas and skills that, when mellowed by your understanding, experiences, and a lot of good common sense, will help you create a nurturing environment for children's social growth. We have not attempted to "teach" other important considerations, especially love, respect, and compassion for children. Yet these things, we feel, are extremely important to our effectiveness. It is our hope that you will combine the techniques offered in this guide with a personal desire to help children in a loving way.

References

Barclay, J.R. Interest patterns associated with measures of social desirability. *Personality Guidance Journal*, 1966, *45*, 56-60.

Berler, E.S., Gross, A.M., & Drabman, R.S. Social skills training with children: Proceed with caution. *Journal of Applied Behavior Analysis*, 1982, *15*, 41-53.

Cartledge, G., & Milburn, J.F. (Eds.). *Teaching social skills to children*. New York: Pergamon Press, 1980.

Cooke, T.P., & Apolloni, T. Developing positive social-emotional behaviors: A study of training and generalization effects. *Journal of Applied Behavior Analysis*, 1976, *9*, 65-78.

Cowen, E.L., Pederson, A., Babigian, H., Izzo, L.D., & Trost, M.A. Long-term follow-up of early detected vulnerable children. *Journal of Consulting and Clinical Psychology*, 1973, *41*, 438-446.

Gambrill, E.D. *Behavior modification: Handbook of assessment, intervention, and evaluation*. San Francisco: Jossey-Bass, 1977.

Greenwood, C., Walker, H., & Hops, H. Issues in social interaction/withdrawal assessment. *Exceptional Children*, 1977, *43*, 490-499.

Guinouard, D.E., & Rychlak, J.F. Personality correlates of sociometric popularity in elementary school children. *Personality Guidance Journal*, 1962, *40*, 438-442.

Hersen, M., & Bellack, A.S. Assessment of social skills. In A.R. Ciminero, K.S. Calhoun, & H.E. Adams (Eds.), *Handbook for behavioral assessment*. New York: Wiley, 1977.

Hops, H., & Greenwood, C.R. Social skills deficit. In E.J. Mash & L.G. Terdal (Eds.), *Behavioral assessment of childhood disorders*. New York: Guilford Press, 1981.

Jackson, D.A. *The effects of training in social competence: Program evaluation and replication*. Unpublished manuscript, 1982. (Available from the author, Social Effectiveness Training, P.O. Box 6664, Reno, Nev. 89513.)

Jackson, D.A., Jackson, N.F., Monroe, C., & Wilkins, C. *Social effectiveness training: The acquisition and generalization of survival skills by socially handicapped children*. Paper presented at the Association for Advancement of Behavior Therapy Convention, San Francisco, December 1979. (Available from the authors, Social Effectiveness Training, P.O. Box 6664, Reno, Nev. 89513.)

Jackson, D.A., Jackson, N.F., Monroe, C., & Wilkins, C. *Social effectiveness training: Training and empirical assessment of affective behavior*. Paper presented at the Association for Advancement of Behavior Therapy Convention, New York City, November 1980. (Available from the authors, Social Effectiveness Training, P.O. Box 6664, Reno, Nev. 89513.)

Jackson, N.F. *Consumer input for program goals: Social skills for children*. Paper presented at the Western Conference on Humanistic Approaches in Behavior Modification, Las Vegas, March 1978. (Available from the author, Social Effectiveness Training, P.O. Box 6664, Reno, Nev. 89513.)

Jackson, N.F., Jackson, D.A., & Monroe, C. Why didn't they teach me this before? *Journal of Staff Development*, 1981, *2*, 55-69.

Kornrich, M. *Underachievement*. Springfield, Ill.: Charles C. Thomas, 1965.

LaGreca, A.M., & Santogrossi, D.A. Social skills training with elementary school students: A behavioral group approach. *Journal of Consulting and Clinical Psychology*, 1980, *48*, 220-227.

Laughlin, F. *The peer status of sixth- and seventh-grade children*. New York: Bureau of Publications, Teacher's College, Columbia University, 1954.

Maloney, D.M., Phillips, E.L., Fixsen, D.L., & Wolf, M.M. Training techniques for staff in group homes for juvenile offenders: An analysis. *Criminal Justice and Behavior*, 1975, *2*, 195-216.

Miller, L.C. *Louisville behavior checklist*. Los Angeles: Western Psychological Services, 1977.

Morris, H.H. Aggressive behavior disorders in children: A follow-up study. *American Journal of Psychiatry*, 1956, *112*, 991-997.

Phillips, E.L., Phillips, E.A., Fixsen, D.L., & Wolf, M.M. *The teaching-family handbook*. Lawrence, Kans.: Bureau of Child Research, University of Kansas, 1974.

Porterfield, O.V., & Schlichting, G.F. Peer status and reading achievement. *Journal of Educational Research*, 1961, *54*, 291-297.

Roff, M., Sells, B., & Golden, M.M. *Social adjustment and personality development in children*. Minneapolis: University of Minnesota Press, 1972.

Ross, A.O. *Psychological aspects of learning disabilities and reading disorders*. New York: McGraw-Hill, 1976.

Schilder, P. The psychogenesis of alcoholism. *Quarterly Journal of Studies on Alcohol*, 1941, *2*, 277-292.

Ullmann, C.A. Teachers, peers, and tests as predictors of adjustment. *Journal of Educational Psychology*, 1957, *48*, 257-267.

Van Hasselt, V.B., Hersen, M., Whitehill, M.B., & Bellack, A.S. Social skill assessment and training for children: An evaluative review. *Behavior Research and Therapy*, 1979, *17*, 413-437.

Zigler, E., & Phillips, L. Social competence and the process reactive distinction in psychopathology. *Journal of Abnormal and Social Psychology*, 1961, *65*, 215-222.

Appendix A

The Consumer Satisfaction Scale

Consumer Satisfaction Scale
(Pre) (Post)

Please circle one: Mother   Father   Teacher   Consultant   Other: _____
Also circle Pre or Post.   (specify)

Child: _____ Date: _____

Please indicate your satisfaction with the extent to which the child shows, or does not show, each behavior. Please circle only one number per item that best describes your opinion.

For example, a child who does not throw things might be rated as follows on this sample item.

A.   Throwing items. That is, the child forcefully sends objects at another   1 2 3 4 5 6 ⑦
       person or object.

Please circle only one number per item.

Completely dissatisfied
Dissatisfied
Slightly dissatisfied
Neither satisfied nor dissatisfied
Slightly satisfied
Satisfied
Completely satisfied

1. Verbal abuse. For example, child uses words or laughter to hurt   1 2 3 4 5 6 7
    or frighten others.

2. Doing what is asked. That is, child obeys without delaying or   1 2 3 4 5 6 7
    complaining.

3. Listening well. For example, child can accurately repeat what   1 2 3 4 5 6 7
    was told.

4. Engaging in conversations. For example, child starts conversations   1 2 3 4 5 6 7
    with others or maintains conversations by actively participating.

5. Eye contact. That is, child looks right at the other person during   1 2 3 4 5 6 7
    a conversation.

6. Friendliness. For example, child smiles and shows concern for others   1 2 3 4 5 6 7
    by asking about them.

7. Kindness and respect. That is, child treats others in a compassionate, 1 2 3 4 5 6 7
    respectful manner.

8. Problem solving. That is, child sees alternatives in problem   1 2 3 4 5 6 7
    situations.

9. Accepting responsibility. That is, child accepts consequences of   1 2 3 4 5 6 7
    his/her actions without blaming others or making excuses.

10. Sincerity and openness. That is, child is frank and able to express   1 2 3 4 5 6 7
    feelings.

101

	Completely dissatisfied	Dissatisfied	Slightly dissatisfied	Neither satisfied nor dissatisfied	Slightly satisfied	Satisfied	Completely satisfied
11. Compromising. For example, child weighs his/her own needs *and* those of the other person to find a solution acceptable to both.	1	2	3	4	5	6	7
12. Accepting criticism. That is, child listens to others' opinions and uses constructive criticism.	1	2	3	4	5	6	7
13. Complaining. That is, child whines, argues, or protests.	1	2	3	4	5	6	7
14. Self-confidence. That is, child feels self-assured and seems to like himself/herself.	1	2	3	4	5	6	7
15. Assertiveness. For example, child stands up for his/her rights by expressing his/her needs.	1	2	3	4	5	6	7
16. Dishonesty. That is, child lies, cheats, or exaggerates.	1	2	3	4	5	6	7
17. Reacting violently. For example, child becomes aggressive at small provocations.	1	2	3	4	5	6	7
18. Physical abuse. That is, child physically hurts people or things.	1	2	3	4	5	6	7
19. Positiveness. That is, child shows appreciation and gives compliments.	1	2	3	4	5	6	7
20. Accepting compliments. For example, child receives compliments without becoming nervous, embarrassed, or arrogant.	1	2	3	4	5	6	7
21. Sense of humor. That is, child is witty or seems to enjoy joking with others.	1	2	3	4	5	6	7
22. Bossiness and self-centeredness. That is, child seems to think only of himself/herself and tells others what to do.	1	2	3	4	5	6	7
23. Demanding. For example, child is insistent about getting help or attention from others.	1	2	3	4	5	6	7
24. Giving up easily. That is, child avoids new tasks or responsibilities.	1	2	3	4	5	6	7
25. Cooperation. That is, child works with others to reach a goal.	1	2	3	4	5	6	7

Please add any comments regarding particular areas.

_____

_____

_____

_____

Appendix B

Answers for Activities

Answers to Activity 2

Write Jason's target behaviors in the spaces below:

1. I follow directions.
2. I have a good attitude.
3. I ask, not tell.
4. I take responsibility for myself.

Answers to Activity 3

Target Behavior Worksheet

I, Jason, agree to work on improving my social skills by doing the following things:

1. I follow directions

which means I: usc a pleasant face and voice,

look at the person giving the directions,

say OK, start to do what was asked right away, and

do it satisfactorily.

2. I have a good attitude

which means I: use a pleasant face and voice, and

look at the person.

3. I ask, not tell

which means I: use a pleasant face and voice,

use please and thank you,

ask, using a question, and

accept "no" as an answer.

4. I take responsibility for myself

which means I: use a pleasant face and voice,

answer questions honestly,

make no excuses, and

accept consequences with a good attitude.

Answers to Activity 4

Asking Nicely

To ask nicely, you:

1. Look at the other person.
2. Make the request with a pleasant face and voice.
3. Use "please."
4. Accept "no" as an answer.

Lining Up

To line up, you:
1. Walk to the door.
2. Keep a quiet voice.
3. Face forward.
4. Keep hands to self.

Getting a Drink

To get a drink in this class, you:
1. Ask teacher's permission.
2. Walk quietly to fountain.
3. Keep water in mouth.
4. Return to seat immediately.

Participating in a Group Discussion

To participate in a group discussion, you:
1. Keep a quiet mouth.
2. Raise hand.
3. Wait to be called on.
4. Keep on the topic of conversation.

Answers to Activity 5

Situation:

You are in a group setting. One *child* is picking up objects off the floor and playing with them.

A correct behavior here is: child is with the group.

The incorrect behavior here is: child is disruptive.

The complete correct behavior here would be: child attends to speaker with still body.

Situation:

During the lesson *one of the children* makes noises such as obtrusive throat clearing, singing, and belching.

A correct behavior here is: child is with the group.

The incorrect behavior here is: child is disruptive.

The complete correct behavior here would be: child attends to speaker with quiet voice.

Situation:

You give one child directions to set up the snack. Another *child* who is working on bossiness-type behaviors says, "Oh, I'll do it Charles, I'll do it with you, let me help!"

A correct behavior here is: child wants to help.

The incorrect behavior here is: child "tells."

The complete correct behavior here would be: child "asks" or lets others do things.

Situation:

Two children are playing together, and one *child* impatiently says to the other in a harsh tone of voice, "It's your turn now!"

A correct behavior here is: child offers other his turn.

The incorrect behavior here is: child uses unpleasant voice.

The complete correct behavior here would be: child offers turn with a pleasant voice.

Situation:

A child is giving Positive Feedback to another child. The *child* giving the feedback tells the other one a specific event that was positive, uses a pleasant tone of voice, but has a grouchy-looking face.

A correct behavior here is: child gives Positive Feedback.

The incorrect behavior here is: child has unpleasant face.

The complete correct behavior here would be: child gives Positive Feedback with pleasant face and voice.

Situation:

You are giving instructions for the children to clean up paints after activity time and go to the circle. One *child* says, in a nice voice, "In a minute."

A correct behavior here is: child speaks with pleasant voice.

The incorrect behavior here is: child doesn't follow directions immediately.

The complete correct behavior here would be: child follows directions immediately.

Situation:

You are giving directions to a *child* who responds by slamming things around and saying, "Oh, all right!" When you say to the child, "It would be better if you followed my directions with a good attitude," the child says, "But I was, I had a good attitude, I did what you said!"

A correct behavior here is: child says, "All right."

The incorrect behavior here is: child makes excuses and has a bad attitude.

The complete correct behavior here would be: child follows directions, listens, gives no excuses, and

has a good attitude.

Situation:

On the playground a really withdrawn *child* is standing on the fringes watching other children play.

A correct behavior here is: child watches peers.

The incorrect behavior here is: child doesn't join in.

The complete correct behavior here would be: child joins peers at play.

Situation:

In the group you prompt for Positive Feedback following a role play. One *child* volunteers appropriately, you call on him, and he says, "I hiked to the top of a mountain last night."

A correct behavior here is: child volunteers appropriately.

The incorrect behavior here is: child gives off-topic answer.

The complete correct behavior here would be: child volunteers with on-topic answer.

107

Situation:

During game time you prompt the children to go over and choose a game and play together. One *child* turns to you and says, "I want to play with you, Teacher."

A correct behavior here is: child chooses a partner.

The incorrect behavior here is: child doesn't follow directions.

The complete correct behavior here would be: child follows directions by playing with peers.

Situation:

The group is preparing for a circle time. Children are sitting in the circle quietly, and one *child* approaches you and sits on your lap.

A correct behavior here is: child comes to group.

The incorrect behavior here is: child doesn't sit with others.

The complete correct behavior here would be: child joins group and sits with others.

Situation:

It is snack time, and the children are having a conversation. One *child* who is sitting in the middle of the group is watching the other children, nodding her head, but not saying anything.

A correct behavior here is: child listens to others talk.

The incorrect behavior here is: child doesn't actively join in.

The complete correct behavior here would be: child listens and actively joins in with peers.

Answers to Activity 8: Vignette 1

1. Teacher made a statement that was *positive*.   (Yes)   No

   The teacher said, "Good work, boys."

2. Teacher made a statement that was *specific*.   Yes   (No)

   The teacher should have said, "Good cooperating" or "Good helping."

3. Teacher made the statement *immediately after* the appropriate behavior.   (Yes)   No

   The teacher did not hesitate.

4. Teacher made a statement that was *true*.   (Yes)   No

   The children were working together well.
   The teacher recognized that.

Answers to Activity 8: Vignette 2

1. Teacher made a statement that was *positive*.   (Yes)   No

   The teacher made a positive statement.

2. Teacher made a statement that was *specific*. Yes (No)

The teacher should have said something specific about the cooperation.

3. Teacher made the statement *immediately after* the appropriate behavior. (Yes) No

The timing was OK, but the statement should have related to the cooperation.

4. Teacher made a statement that was *true*. (Yes) No

This may or may not be true; however, the teacher should have focused on Billy's behavior, not quality judgments about him.

Answers to Activity 8: Vignette 3

1. Teacher made a statement that was *positive*. (Yes) No

The *first* part of the teacher's statement was positive. Nothing more needed to be said.

2. Teacher made a statement that was *specific*. (Yes) No

The teacher said, "Thanks for *helping* Shawn."

3. Teacher made the statement *immediately after* the appropriate behavior. (Yes) No

The teacher did not hesitate.

4. Teacher made a statement that was *true*. (Yes) No

Billy was helping Shawn, therefore, the teacher's statement was true.

Answers to Activity 13: Vignette 1

1. Teacher *ignored* the child behaving inappropriately. Yes (No)

The teacher should not have said anything to Susie.

2. Teacher *attended* to and praised the child behaving appropriately. (Yes) No

The teacher gave Positive Feedback to Johnny.

3. Teacher *praised* the child when the behavior became appropriate. (Yes) No

The teacher gave Positive Feedback to Susie when she began to cooperate.

Answers to Activity 13: Vignette 2

1. Teacher *ignored* the child behaving inappropriately. (Yes) No

   The teacher did not attend to Susie.

2. Teacher *attended* to and praised the child behaving appropriately. (Yes) No

   The teacher gave Positive Feedback to Johnny.

3. Teacher *praised* the child when the behavior became appropriate. Yes (No)

   The teacher should have given Positive Feedback to Susie
   instead of saying something negative.

Answers to Activity 13: Vignette 3

1. Teacher *ignored* the child behaving inappropriately. Yes (No)

   The teacher should have ignored Susie.

2. Teacher *attended* to and praised the child behaving appropriately. Yes (No)

   The teacher should have given Johnny Positive Feedback
   for following directions.

3. Teacher *praised* the child when the behavior became appropriate. (Yes) No

   The teacher used a general praise statement but could
   have improved it with Positive Feedback.

Answers to Activity 18: Vignette 1

1. Teacher stopped the interaction by *saying something positive*
   that was related to the situation. (Yes) No

   The teacher gave Positive Feedback for initiating a conversation.

2. Teacher asked the child for an *alternative way of behaving*. If the
   child didn't know, the teacher *verbalized* or *modeled* one and had
   the child repeat it. Yes (No)

   The teacher should have asked for an alternative behavior.

3. Teacher asked the child to *practice* the appropriate behavior. Yes (No)

   The teacher should have required the child to practice
   while the teacher observed.

4. Teacher gave the child *Positive Feedback* for *any* improvement. Yes (No)

   Had the child practiced, the teacher could have given
   Positive Feedback.

5. Teacher gave the child *homework*. Yes No

The teacher said, "Please do that from now on."

Answers to Activity 18: Vignette 2

1. Teacher stopped the interaction by *saying something positive* that was related to the situation. Yes No

The teacher should have made a positive statement about initiating a conversation.

2. Teacher asked the child for an *alternative way of behaving*. If the child didn't know, the teacher *verbalized* or *modeled* one and had the child repeat it. Yes No

The teacher said, "How could you do that?"

3. Teacher asked the child to *practice* the appropriate behavior. Yes No

The teacher said, "You can show me."

4. Teacher gave the child *Positive Feedback* for *any* improvement. Yes No

The teacher said, "What a nice way to join our conversation!"

5. Teacher gave the child *homework*. Yes No

The teacher said, "The next time you want to interrupt a conversation . . ."

Answers to Activity 18: Vignette 3

1. Teacher stopped the interaction by *saying something positive* that was related to the situation. Yes No

The teacher gave Positive Feedback for initiating a conversation.

2. Teacher asked the child for an *alternative way of behaving*. If the child didn't know, the teacher *verbalized* or *modeled* one and had the child repeat it. Yes No

The teacher said, "How could you do that?"

3. Teacher asked the child to *practice* the appropriate behavior. Yes No

The teacher should have asked the child to practice.

4. Teacher gave the child *Positive Feedback* for *any* improvement. Yes No

Had the child practiced, the teacher could have given Positive Feedback.

5. Teacher gave the child *homework*. Yes No

The teacher should have said, "The next time you want to interrupt a conversation . . ."

111

Answers to Activity 23: Vignette 1

1. Teacher used a *calm voice* and *eye contact*. Yes (No)

    The teacher did use eye contact but should have also used a calm voice.

2. Teacher made a *brief statement* about the behavior that is desired (e.g., "You need to keep your hands to yourself"). Yes (No)

    The teacher should have said, "You need to have still hands and look at the speaker."

3. Teacher *watched for the appropriate behavior* and *praised the child*. Yes (No)

    The teacher should have specified the expected behavior, then watched for it, and praised the child when it occurred.

Answers to Activity 23: Vignette 2

1. Teacher used a *calm voice* and *eye contact*. (Yes) No

    The teacher used a calm voice and eye contact.

2. Teacher made a *brief statement* about the behavior that is desired (e.g., "You need to keep your hands to yourself"). Yes (No)

    The teacher initially made a brief statement, but then rationalized, making it too long.

3. Teacher *watched for the appropriate behavior* and *praised the child*. Yes (No)

    The child eventually followed directions, and the teacher should have praised him.

Answers to Activity 23: Vignette 3

1. Teacher used a *calm voice* and *eye contact*. (Yes) No

    The teacher used a calm voice and eye contact.

2. Teacher made a *brief statement* about the behavior that is desired (e.g., "You need to keep your hands to yourself"). (Yes) No

    The teacher said, "You need to keep your hands still in your lap."

3. Teacher *watched for the appropriate behavior* and *praised the child*. Yes (No)

    The child followed directions, and the teacher should have praised him.

Answers for Activity 28: Vignette 1

1. Teacher *removed the child* to the Sit and Watch chair, calmly saying, "_____, you need to sit and watch how the other children (*the desired behavior*, e.g., work quietly without making noise)."   Yes   (No)

   The teacher removed the child to Sit and Watch, but should have said, "Jim, you need to watch the others paying attention and being serious."

2. Teacher *timed the child's wait* for *2* minutes.   (Yes)   No

   The teacher noted the time before returning to the group.

3. Teacher *praised others* for appropriate behavior.   Yes   (No)

   The teacher should have given Positive Feedback to the other group members for paying attention and being serious.

4. After 2 minutes, the teacher *went to the child* and *gave Positive Feedback*, calmly saying, "_____, you've been sitting quietly with your hands still."   (Yes)   No

   The teacher went to the child after 2 minutes and gave him Positive Feedback for sitting still.

5. Teacher *had the child name the inappropriate behavior*, saying, "You need to tell me why you're in Sit and Watch." (If the child couldn't name the misbehavior, the teacher stated it and had the child repeat it.) Then the teacher *said*, "Right."   (Yes)   No

   The teacher had the child name the inappropriate behavior and praised him for naming it.

6. Teacher *had the child name the appropriate behavior*, saying, "What do you need to do when you get back to the group?" (If the child couldn't name the correct behavior, the teacher stated it and had the child repeat it.) Then the teacher *said*, "Good for you. You can come back to the group now."   Yes   (No)

   The teacher should have had the child name the appropriate behavior and praised him for naming it.

7. After the child returned to the group, the teacher *watched for the correct behavior* and *gave Positive Feedback for the child's correct behavior*.   Yes   (No)

   Once the child was back in the group, the teacher should have watched for the appropriate behavior and given Positive Feedback.

113

Answers for Activity 28: Vignette 2

1. Teacher *removed the child* to the Sit and Watch chair, calmly saying, "_____, you need to sit and watch how the other children (*the desired behavior*, e.g., work quietly without making noise)."   **(Yes)**   No

   The teacher removed the child to Sit and Watch, and said, "Jim, you need to . . ."

2. Teacher *timed the child's wait* for 2 minutes.   **(Yes)**   No

   The teacher noted the time before returning to the group.

3. Teacher *praised others* for appropriate behavior.   Yes   **(No)**

   The teacher should have given Positive Feedback to the other group members for paying attention and being serious.

4. After 2 minutes, the teacher *went to the child* and *gave Positive Feedback*, calmly saying, "_____, you've been sitting quietly with your hands still."   Yes   **(No)**

   The teacher went to the child after 2 minutes, but should have given the child Positive Feedback for sitting quietly and having still hands while in Sit and Watch.

5. Teacher *had the child name the inappropriate behavior*, saying, "You need to tell me why you're in Sit and Watch." (If the child couldn't name the misbehavior, the teacher stated it and had the child repeat it.) Then the teacher *said*, "Right."   Yes   **(No)**

   The teacher had the child name the inappropriate behavior but should have praised him for naming it.

6. Teacher *had the child name the appropriate behavior*, saying, "What do you need to do when you get back to the group?" (If the child couldn't name the correct behavior, the teacher stated it and had the child repeat it.) Then the teacher *said*, "Good for you. You can come back to the group now."   **(Yes)**   No

   The teacher had the child name the appropriate behavior, praised him, and then brought him back to the group.

7. After the child returned to the group, the teacher *watched for the correct behavior* and *gave Positive Feedback for the child's correct behavior*.   Yes   **(No)**

   Once the child was back in the group, the teacher should have watched for the appropriate behavior and given Positive Feedback.

Answers for Activity 28: Vignette 3

1. Teacher *removed the child* to the Sit and Watch chair, calmly saying, "_____, you need to sit and watch how the other children (*the desired behavior*, e.g., work quietly without making noise)."

   Yes   (No)

   The teacher removed the child to Sit and Watch, but should have said, "Jim, you need to watch the others paying attention and being serious."

2. Teacher *timed the child's wait* for 2 minutes.

   (Yes)   No

   The teacher noted the time before returning to the group.

3. Teacher *praised others* for appropriate behavior.

   Yes   (No)

   The teacher should have given Positive Feedback to the other group members for paying attention and being serious.

4. After 2 minutes, the teacher *went to the child* and *gave Positive Feedback*, calmly saying, "_____, you've been sitting quietly with your hands still."

   Yes   (No)

   The teacher went to the child after 2 minutes but should have given Positive Feedback for sitting quietly and having still hands while in Sit and Watch.

5. Teacher *had the child name the inappropriate behavior*, saying, "You need to tell me why you're in Sit and Watch." (If the child couldn't name the misbehavior, the teacher stated it and had the child repeat it.) Then the teacher *said*, "Right."

   Yes   (No)

   The teacher had the child name the inappropriate behavior but should have praised him for naming it.

6. Teacher *had the child name the appropriate behavior*, saying, "What do you need to do when you get back to the group?" (If the child couldn't name the correct behavior, the teacher stated it and had the child repeat it.) Then the teacher *said*, "Good for you. You can come back to the group now."

   Yes   (No)

   The teacher should have had the child name the complete appropriate behavior and then praised him for naming it.

7. After the child returned to the group, the teacher *watched for the correct behavior* and *gave Positive Feedback for the child's correct behavior*.

   Yes   (No)

   Once the child was back in the group, the teacher should have watched for the appropriate behavior and given Positive Feedback.

115

Answers for Activity 30

1. You have just used Sit and Watch with a child in your group who refused to role play. What should you do when you bring him back to the group?

   Praise him for appropriate group behaviors and have him role play.

2. A child in your group just pinched another child. This is the first time this child has done anything of this sort. What Teaching Strategy would you use? Give your rationale.

   Before using Sit and Watch, I would try the Direct Prompt for keeping hands to self because this is not the child's typical behavior.

3. What would you change about this physical arrangement?

   The Sit and Watch chair should be moved to the other side of the group so that the teacher can see it while with the group.

Sit and Watch
chair

teacher

About the Authors

Nancy and Don Jackson and Cathy Monroe were primarily responsible for the development of Social Effectiveness Training (S.E.T.), originally done as a handicapped children's model program. Over the last 8 years, they have been refining and applying S.E.T. with a variety of client populations within diverse settings.

Nancy Jackson supervised the development of the program's curriculum, Teaching Strategies, and teacher training procedures. In addition to her social skills work with children, she has developed expertise in teacher and parent training and has conducted numerous workshops and classes in these areas. Nancy holds the M.Ed. degree in special education from the University of Nevada, Reno. Her experience includes classroom teaching with various emotionally and mentally handicapped populations, and educational consultation. She is currently a private contractor and Program Coordinator for the Institute for Social Effectiveness Training, a nonprofit educational corporation providing training and consultation to families and professionals.

Don Jackson has the M.A. degree in psychology from Western Michigan University and the Ph.D. in educational psychology from the University of Utah. While an Adjunct Assistant Professor in the Department of Human Development at the University of Kansas, he conducted educational research and interventions with schools throughout the nation. In Reno, he was Project Director for the Social Effectiveness Training program and Education Director for Children's Behavioral Services, a state mental health agency. His publications have dealt primarily with educational treatment programs for children and youth with special needs. Currently, Dr. Jackson is Community Psychologist for Northern Nevada Mental Retardation Services, an adjunct faculty member of the College of Education, University of Nevada, Reno, and President of the Institute for Social Effectiveness Training.

Cathy Monroe was teacher, program developer, and teacher trainer for the S.E.T. developmental project. Her teaching provided a model of how to work effectively with children; the program thus reflects the lessons learned by watching and listening to her. Cathy received the M.Ed. in special education from the University of Nevada, Reno. She has experience in programs for educationally handicapped, mentally handicapped, and regular students, and has conducted workshops and classes on S.E.T. for parents and professionals. She is a consultant for the Institute for Social Effectiveness Training.